October 20–24, 2014
Portland, Oregon, USA

I0053553

Association for Computing Machinery

Advancing Computing as a Science & Profession

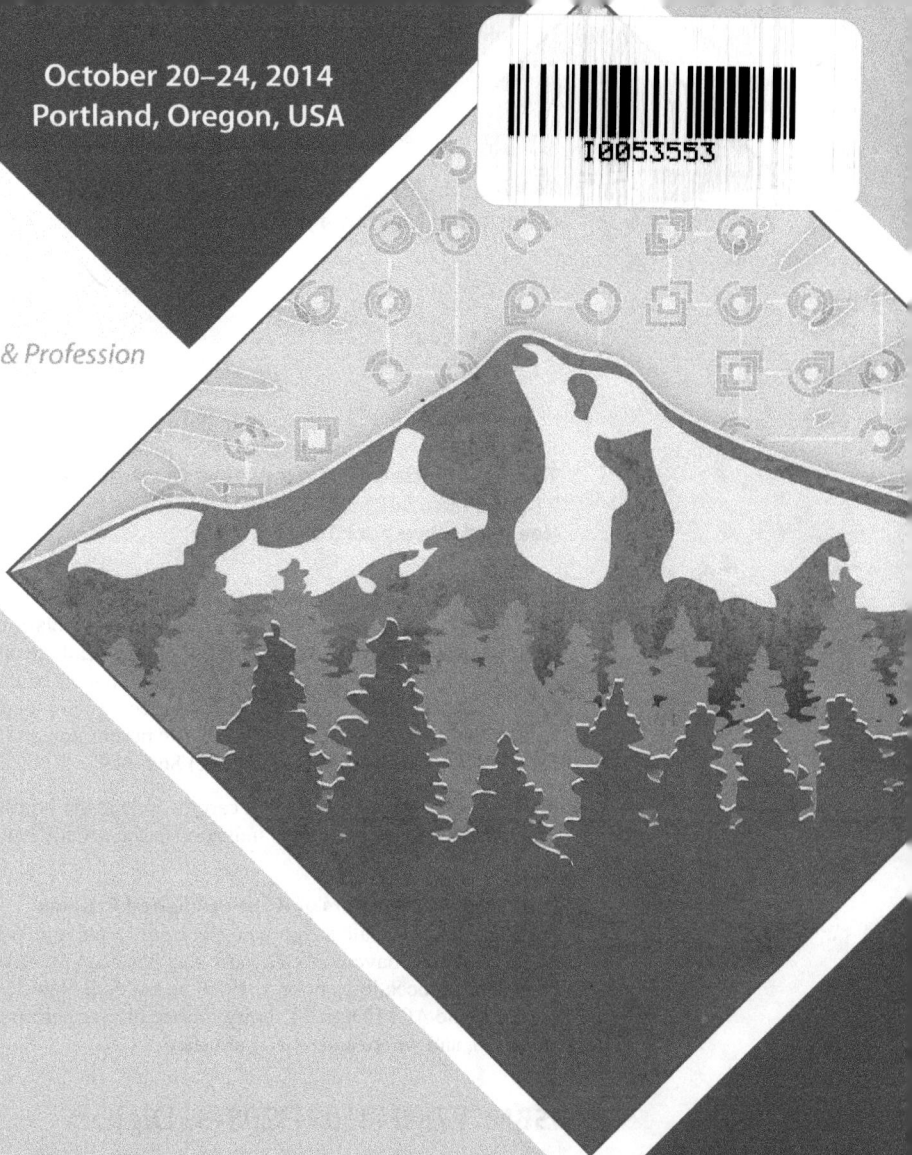

SPLASH'14

Companion Publication of the 2014 ACM SIGPLAN
Conference on Systems, Programming, and Applications: Software for Humanity

Sponsored by:
ACM SIGPLAN

In cooperation with:
ACM SIGAda

Supported by:
Microsoft Research, Oracle Labs, IBM Research, Hewlett-Packard, Goldman Sachs, Google, & CRC Press

Association for
Computing Machinery

Advancing Computing as a Science & Profession

The Association for Computing Machinery
2 Penn Plaza, Suite 701
New York, New York 10121-0701

ISBN: 978-1-4503-3208-8 (Digital)

ISBN: 978-1-4503-3382-5 (Print)

Additional copies may be ordered prepaid from:

ACM Order Department
PO Box 30777
New York, NY 10087-0777, USA

Phone: 1-800-342-6626 (USA and Canada)
+1-212-626-0500 (Global)
Fax: +1-212-944-1318
E-mail: acmhelp@acm.org
Hours of Operation: 8:30 am – 4:30 pm ET

Printed in the USA

Welcome from the SPLASH 2014 General Chair

On behalf of the whole SPLASH organizing committee, I am delighted to welcome you (back!) to Portland, Oregon, for SPLASH 2014. While OOPSLA has a long and storied history, starting in Portland in 1986, we took the plunge into SPLASH only in 2010, when we started using that name for the umbrella venue that encompasses *OOPSLA*, *Onward!*, *Onward! Essays*, *Wavefront*, and the *Dynamic Languages Symposium*, as well as the lively collection of keynotes, demonstrations, tutorials, workshops and smaller symposia that make SPLASH unique.

In 1986 it was hard to imagine that object-orientation would become the dominant technology for the software industry. With that dominance has come the recognition that objects are not the only viable technology, nor even the best technology for all situations. Thus, SPLASH now embraces all aspects of software construction and delivery, as well as programming languages, and software engineering. *OOPSLA* continues to present research that pushes the edge of what objects can do. *Onward!* encompasses everything to do with programming and software, including software process, development methods, languages, communities, and applications. We hope that *Onward!* remains more open than other conferences to not yet well-proven ideas.

For the first time, SPLASH is co-locating with HILT, the annual SIGAda conference on High Integrity Language Technology. SPLASH-E for educators is in its second year, and Kathi Fissler has put together an interesting program that brings together research in learning and developments in software technology. Some other familiar symposia, like SLE and PLoP, are elsewhere this year, but are likely to be back in 2015.

Wavefront should be about the practice of software development. It's always been difficult to get practicing software engineers to write papers: the incentives of the software industry reward running code, not academic papers. This year we tried something a little different: soliciting talks rather than papers. The small size of *Wavefront* is a clear indicator that we don't yet have the right formula; you are invited to share your ideas on how to re-invent Wavefront with the SPLASH Steering committee.

In contrast, the *Dynamic Languages Symposium* continues to attract a lively collection of submissions. Indeed, I am tempted to argue that DLS represents both the cutting edge of innovation in OO and the continued evolution of some of the far-out ideas from the 1980s — ideas that the far greater speed and memory capacity of today's hardware have enabled us to take to their logical conclusion.

I'm especially pleased to welcome three very distinguished keynote speakers: Gary McGraw, Peter Norvig, and Bret Victor. Security, or rather the lack of it, has made headlines this year — as it does every year — with the usual batch of embarrassing security breaches, but also the interesting case of the Heartbleed vulnerability, which helped to make clear that opening software to the scrutiny of many eyes, while helpful, does not itself solve the security problem. On Wednesday, Gary McGraw of Cigital will talk about transitioning (security) technologies from the lab into practice, and will also participate in a panel on security.

On Thursday, Peter Norvig of Google asks us to consider whether machine learning could, or should, make traditional programming obsolete. Just as we routinely use machine learning algorithms to capture the complex decision-making that goes into recognizing human speech or faces in photographs, might we not use those same algorithms to capture the decision-making that goes into, say, writing a compiler? On Friday, Bret Victor challenges us to think about the costs as well as the benefits of static, written notations. Computing technology offers us the possibility to represent ideas dynamically rather statically:

does this offer a better cost/benefit ratio? Or, to put it another way: could the "movie" of your program replace the program text?

Organizing SPLASH is a lot of work. My job has been made possible only by the collaboration of a large number — 28 at last count — of organizing committee members and subcommittee chairs, of the SPLASH steering committee, of Carole Mann and her registration team, and of our conference manager, Annabel Satin. I owe every one of them a debt of thanks. Financial support from a number of corporations has saved me from some hard choices. However, in some sense, the real thanks go to you, the members for the SPLASH community, who continue to look to this conference as a stimulating place to come and present the latest research and debate contentious issues. The team of volunteers who put on SPLASH every year is powered by your energy. I am confident that so long — but only so long — as you find SPLASH an exciting place to interact with others, SPLASH will continue to be here for you.

Andrew P. Black
SPLASH'14 General Chair
Portland State University,
Portland, Oregon, USA

Table of Contents

Panels

Student Research Competition

Posters

Wavefront

Co-located Workshop Summaries

Post Conference Workshop Summaries

Author Index

SPLASH 2014 Organization

General Chair:	Andrew Black *(Portland State University, USA)*
OOPSLA Program Chair:	Todd Millstein *(University of California, Los Angeles, USA)*
Onward! Program Chair:	Shriram Krishnamurthi *(Brown University, USA)*
Onward! Essays Program Chair:	Bernd Brügge *(Technische Universität München, Germany)*
DLS Program Chair:	Laurie Tratt *(King's College London, UK)*
Treasurer & Conference Manager:	Annabel Satin *(Petit Canard Kitchen, UK)*
Publications Chair:	Joseph N. Ruskiewicz *(eBay and Portland State University, USA)*
Tutorials Chair:	James Noble *(Victoria University of Wellington, New Zealand)*
Demos Chair:	Floreal Morandat *(Enseirb-Matmeca and LaBRI, France)*
Posters Co-chairs:	K R Jayaram *(IBM Research, USA)* and Nick Sumner *(Simon Fraser University, Canada)*
SPLASH-E:	Kathi Fisler *(Worcester Polytechnic Institute, USA)*
Workshops Co-Chairs:	Stephanie Balzer and Du Li *(Carnegie Mellon University, USA)*
Wavefront Co-Chairs:	Dennis Mancl *(Alcatel-Lucent)* and Dave Archer *(Galois, USA)*
Student Research Competition:	Işıl Dillig *(University of Texas, Austin, USA)* and Sam Guyer *(Tufts University, USA)*
Student Volunteer Captains:	Jonathan Bell *(Columbia University, USA)* and Darya Kurilova *(Carnegie Mellon University, USA)*
Web Technology Chair:	Eelco Visser *(Delft University of Technology, The Netherlands)*
Publicity & Web Content Chair:	Craig Anslow *(University of Calgary, Canada)*
Student Mentoring Co-Chairs:	Carlos Jensen and Danny Dig *(Oregon State University, USA)*
Panels:	Steve Fraser *(Independent Consultant, USA)*
Mobile App Chair:	Reid Holmes *(University of Waterloo, Canada)*

Student Mentoring Co-Chairs:	Carlos Jensen and Danny Dig *(Oregon State University, USA)*
Doctoral Symposium Chair:	Lukasz Ziarek *(State University of New York, Buffalo, USA)*
SPLASH Steering Committee Chair:	Cristina V. Lopes *(University of California, Irvine, USA)*
SPLASH Steering Committee:	Andrew Black *(Portland State University, USA)*
	William Cook *(University of Texas at Austin, USA)*
	Matt Dwyer *(University of Nebraska, USA)*
	Jonathan Edwards *(MIT, USA)*
	Patrick Eugster *(Purdue University, USA)*
	Kathleen Fisher *(Tufts University, USA)*
	Jeremy Gibbons *(University of Oxford, UK)*
	Robert Hirschfeld *(Hasso-Plattner-Institute, Germany)*
	Tony Hosking *(Purdue University, USA)*
	Gary Leavens *(University of Central Florida, USA)*
	Todd Millstein *(University of California, Los Angeles, USA)*
	Kevin Sullivan *(University of Virginia, USA)*
	Eelco Visser *(Delft University of Technology, The Netherlands)*
	Jan Vitek *(Northeastern University, USA)*

 **SPLASH 2014 Sponsor & Supporters**

Sponsor:

In-cooperation with:  Ada

Gold Supporter: Microsoft Research

Silver Supporter: Oracle Labs

Bronze Supporters: Google™   **IBM Research**

CRC Press
Taylor & Francis Group

we BUILD   Goldman Sachs

Software Security — A Study in Technology Transfer

Gary McGraw
Cigital

Abstract

Where do security technologies come from? Academics propose research and government (sometimes) funds it. Startups move technologies across the "research valley of death" to early adopters. Global corporations make technology widely available by acquiring startups. At every step there are gaps and pitfalls.

Adoption is the acid test of innovation. Idea-generation is perhaps ten per cent of innovation; most of the work is on technology transfer and adoption. Chance plays a big role in creating opportunities (e.g., R&D involves a lot of luck), but a company's success depends on its ability to make opportunities more likely to occur, and to capitalize on those opportunities when they arise. Passionate individuals drive technology transfer more than does process; indeed, some people believe that the original researchers need to be involved all the way along the chain. Prototyping is an important practice, often resulting in "researchware" that proves a concept but is not ready for wide use. Transforming a prototype from the lab to the real-world is a multi-stage, multi-year undertaking.

This talk will use the decade-long evolution of static analysis in code review as a driver for discussion. We'll talk startups, big companies, venture capital, research agencies, and subject-matter expertise. In general, technologists don't appreciate business people enough and business people don't appreciate technology enough. Most successful companies are brilliant at one, but also need to be adequate at the other.

ACM Classification: K.4.4 [Computers and Society] Electronic Commerce—Security; K.6.5 [Management of Computing and Information Systems] Security and Protection—Software Vulnerabilities; D.2.5 [Software Engineering] Testing and Debugging—Static Analysis.

Author Keywords: Technology Transfer; Security; technolgy adoption; static analysis; code review.

Biography

Gary McGraw is the CTO of Cigital, Inc., a software-security consulting firm with headquarters in the Washington, D.C. area and offices throughout the world. He is a globally recognized authority on software security and the author of eight best-selling books on this topic. His titles include Software Security, Exploiting Software, Building Secure Software, Java Security, and Exploiting Online Games; he is also editor of the Addison-Wesley Software Security series. Dr. McGraw has written over 100 peer-reviewed scientific publications, authors a monthly security column for SearchSecurity and Information Security Magazine, and is frequently quoted in the press. Besides serving as a strategic counselor for top business and IT executives, Gary is on the Advisory Boards of Dasient (acquired by Twitter), Fortify Software (acquired by HP), Raven White, Max Financial, Invotas, and Wall+Main. His dual PhD in Cognitive Science and Computer Science is from Indiana University, where he serves on the Dean's Advisory Council for the School of Informatics. Gary served on the IEEE Computer Society Board of Governors and produces the monthly Silver Bullet Security Podcast for IEEE Security & Privacy magazine (syndicated by SearchSecurity).

SPLASH'14, October 20–24, 2014, Portland, Oregon, USA.
ACM 978-1-4503-3208-8/14/10.
http://dx.doi.org/10.1145/2660252.2661745

Machine Learning for Programming

Peter Norvig
Google
pnorvig@google.com

Abstract

If you want to recognize speech or filter out spam emails, you will probably write a machine learning algorithm and will not try to write the whole program using a "traditional" software specification and implementation. There are many examples of successful machine learning solutions, but can we more broadly apply the techniques to most or all software problems, and for most or all programmers, from the novice in their first programming course to the seasoned professional?

ACM Classification: D.2.3 [Coding Tools and Techniques]; I.2.6 [Learning]

Author Keywords: Machine Learning; Programming

Biography

Peter Norvig is a Director of Research at Google Inc. Previously he was head of Google's core search algorithms group, and of NASA Ames's Computational Sciences Division, making him NASA's senior computer scientist. He received the NASA Exceptional Achievement Award in 2001. He has taught at the University of Southern California and the University of California at Berkeley, from which he received a Ph.D. in 1986 and the distinguished alumni award in 2006. He was co-teacher of an Artifical Intelligence class that signed up 160,000 students, helping to kick off the current round of massive open online classes.

His publications include the books Artificial Intelligence: A Modern Approach (the leading textbook in the field), Paradigms of AI Programming: Case Studies in Common Lisp, Verbmobil: A Translation System for Face-to-Face Dialog, and Intelligent Help Systems for UNIX. He is also the author of the Gettysburg Powerpoint Presentation and the world's longest palindromic sentence. He is a fellow of the AAAI, ACM, California Academy of Science and American Academy of Arts & Sciences.

SPLASH'14, October 20–24, 2014, Portland, Oregon, USA.
ACM 978-1-4503-3208-8/14/10.
http://dx.doi.org/10.1145/2660252.2661744

Humane Representation of Thought:
A Trail Map for the 21st Century

Bret Victor

Abstract

New representations of thought — written language, mathematical notation, information graphics, etc — have been responsible for some of the most significant leaps in the progress of civilization, by expanding humanity's collectively-thinkable territory.

But at debilitating cost. These representations, having been invented for static media such as paper, tap into a small subset of human capabilities and neglect the rest. Knowledge work means sitting at a desk, interpreting and manipulating symbols. The human body is reduced to an eye staring at tiny rectangles and fingers on a pen or keyboard.

Like any severely unbalanced way of living, this is crippling to mind and body. But less obviously, and more importantly, it is enormously wasteful of the vast human potential. Human beings naturally have many powerful modes of thinking and understanding. Most are incompatible with static media. In a culture that has contorted itself around the limitations of marks on paper, these modes are undeveloped, unrecognized, or scorned.

We are now seeing the start of a dynamic medium. To a large extent, people today are using this medium merely to emulate and extend static representations from the era of paper, and to further constrain the ways in which the human body can interact with external representations of thought.

But the dynamic medium offers the opportunity to deliberately invent *a humane and empowering form of knowledge work*. We can design dynamic representations which draw on the entire range of human capabilities — all senses, all forms of movement, all forms of understanding — instead of straining a few and atrophying the rest.

This talk suggests how each of the human activities in which thought is externalized (conversing, presenting, reading, writing, etc) can be redesigned around such representations.

ACM Classification:
H.5.0 [Information Interfaces and Presentation]: General

Author Keywords
Dynamic representations

Bio

Bret Victor has designed experimental UI concepts at Apple, interactive data graphics for Al Gore, and musical instruments at Alesis. He's responsible for "Inventing on Principle", "Learnable Programming," "Media for Thinking the Unthinkable," "Up and Down the Ladder of Abstraction," "Magic Ink," and everything else at worrydream.com.

SPLASH 2014 Doctoral Symposium Chairs' Welcome

OCTOBER 19–24

SPLASH

PORTLAND 2014

It is our great pleasure to welcome you to Portland and the 2014 Doctoral Symposium! This year's symposium continues the tradition of providing students with an opportunity for additional feedback and suggestions on their dissertation work, contacts for further interaction, and experience in communicating with other professionals in their field of study. The SPLASH Doctoral Symposium provides students with useful guidance for completing their dissertation research and beginning their research careers.

We are happy to report that the overall quality of this year's submissions was high. Out of a total of 6 proposer applications, the program committee accepted 6 proposals whose topics range from software engineering and HCI to language runtime design.

Beyond the formal program, we hope this year's doctoral symposium will, like its predecessors, be a valuable forum for sharing ideas on the students' research. We are happy that you are able to join us for this exciting doctoral symposium, and hope that the ideas you take home with you will enrich the experience of your students and provide valuable feedback as they prepare to defend their dissertation work. Thank you for being part of this exciting community, and once again, welcome!

Lukasz Ziarek
Chair
SUNY Buffalo

Diagnosing Degenerate Forms in Software

Brian S. Dillon

Naval Surface Warfare Center, Dahlgren Division (NSWCDD)
Virginia Polytechnic Institute and State University
briand81@vt.edu

Abstract

The degeneration of source code due to maintenance is a long known but little understood phenomenon. Currently, researchers face significant logistical challenges when conducting empirical studies and experiments, studying large-scale projects, and characterizing the development and growth of degenerative forms. These logistical challenges can be partially alleviated by developing automated metrics designed to identify degenerate forms. Furthermore, such metrics are essential for targeted refactoring and repairing degenerative forms. This dissertation research investigates a set of metrics targeted at specific degenerate forms common in software. The successful implementation and characterization of such metrics will enable further research in many forms of software maintenance.

Categories and Subject Descriptors D.2.9 [**Software Engineering**]: Management – software quality assurance.

General Terms Measurement, Management, Design, Experimentation.

Keywords software evolution; degeneration; software metrics; diagnostics; refactoring

1. Introduction

Software evolution is a problem long known to computer science and has been addressed by various names, e.g., aging, rot, entropy, erosion. Essentially, software that undergoes maintenance must change over time, and the cumulative effects of those changes create adverse conditions for future maintenance. These adverse conditions eventually make maintenance infeasible. This problem is found in most large-scale, long-lived software projects but is still little understood.

In order to enable further research in this area, improved metrics are required. This dissertation research investigates several metrics that have been designed to identify specific degenerate software forms commonly found in software demonstrating the effects of software evolution. The goal of this research is to characterize the accuracy and effectiveness of these metrics in locating and diagnosing degenerate forms as an aide to future work.

OOPSLA'14, October 20–24, 2014, Portland, Oregon, USA.
ACM 978-1-4503-2585-1/14/10.
http://dx.doi.org/10.1145/2660252.2660255

2. Problem Statement

The costs associated with software degeneration are high. Even with the many man-hours invested to develop a current software baseline, at some point the cost of maintaining degraded software is more than the cost of new development. Three examples from industry were described in [9] where software was abandoned for this reason. These cases indicated the need to abandon new software shortly after it was released and even while it was still under development. Each case was described as requiring a "massive effort," and they concluded "…[r]edeveloping software … is a very expensive and lengthy procedure…." and in the end "was only partly successful." The cost of redevelopment on multiple software products, over many years and by many different developers, is a monumental expenditure that can and must be eliminated.

Up to this point, research into this phenomenon has been dominated by Lehman's eight laws of software evolution [7]. Lehman continued to revise his own laws over the years as his understanding of the phenomenon changed. Researchers in this field tend to agree that software evolution is a naturally occurring, degenerative phenomenon, which is at least partially the product of development practices, resource constraints, and time. Nevertheless, researchers have not done a great deal to characterize the development of these degenerate software forms, principally because of the logistical concerns in carrying out even a limited study of software "in the wild." While there are a large number of strategies for improving software development, there is little empirical evidence to determine how these strategies affect the rate of degeneration.

The lack of empirical studies, according to multiple researchers, is the result of logistical difficulties in producing statistically significant quantities of sample data. Without such samples, it is impossible to draw meaningful conclusions as to a positive or negative effect derived from specific development strategies. Kemerer and Slaughter [6] noted that research of this type requires at least two different data points from two different times. "This," they note, "creates practical difficulties in terms of sustaining support for the [research] project over this period or finding an organization that collects and retains … data or the software artifacts themselves." Researchers are further hampered by their inability to accurately measure the quality of the software without resorting to expert classification. Metrics do exist that point to various characteristics of code, but none give an objective and quantifiable measure of the degeneration that has taken place.

3. Motivation for Dissertation Research

The author's personal motivation to investigate this problem came from his work as a professional developer. That work involved the refactoring of multiple degenerated legacy software products in preparation for new development. This led to first-hand experience with degenerate software forms and knowledge of the current limits of refactoring. Refactoring has had mixed results across the industry as a whole for reasons identified by [2]. They indicate that i) identifying code smells requires a priori knowledge of the code, ii) code smells and refactoring focus on a small subset of code without any planned effect on the whole, and iii) the relative value of code smells is not easily quantified. In short, the value of refactoring is strongly associated with the experience and knowledge of the developer and, even with an experienced developer, manual detection and refactoring of degenerate forms is limited by these same factors.

In order to enable further research in this area and improve the quality of refactoring in general, there is a need for new automated metrics. Researchers are unable to greatly further our understanding of the degeneration phenomenon in general because they are unable to conduct meaningful studies and experiments on large-scale source code. Developers are unable to efficiently locate, identify, and resolve these degenerate forms because they are limited by human experience and speed. Current software metrics, biased toward easily quantifiable characteristics such as method size and nesting loops, are incapable of improving these conditions. While such metrics may or may not indicate areas of concern, they are hardly diagnostic in the strict sense. New metrics must be developed that are objective and yield quantitative results capable of diagnosing and locating degenerate forms more efficiently.

4. Approach

The proposed research will develop just such a set of metrics that can be used to identify and locate specific degenerate forms. Preliminary surveys of degenerate forms were conducted using four source codes developed by diverse groups and in two different languages, C# and Java. During the four refactoring case studies, a list of 24 common degenerate forms was compiled. These degenerate forms include violations of commonly accepted principles of good software engineering, such as encapsulation and interface segregation. Others are related to common areas of concern such as unreachable code, unused variables, incorrectly modified class members, and poorly named variables. All of these were identified in production code and were unidentified by the compiler or other tools.

The author designed new metrics to detect these degenerate forms without a priori knowledge and in a quantifiable and objective way that approximates the classification of an expert human developer. Typically, two or three metrics work cooperatively to identify the degenerate forms. A subset of metrics that cooperatively exposed a large group of degenerate forms was selected for further development and experimentation. The results from the selected metrics are mainly quantifiable rather than merely indicative. With these metrics, it should be possible to track and target degenerate forms where they occur in wild code during refactoring and degeneration research.

The first metric is a novel approach to state. Several degenerate forms are associated with inconsistent state, overly complex state, and co-dependent state variables, but identifying state variables generally requires a human intelligence. The author has created a method that uses the statistical properties of code to determine which variables are likely state variables and which have no effect on the con-

```
public class ClassB
{
    public void Use(int hr, int hnr, int pw)
    {
        int a = hr+pw;<--- found by pmd
        a++;
    }
}

public class ClassA
{
    private int neverUsed;//<--- found by PMD
    private int neverRead;//<--- found by PMD
    private int neverWritten;//<--- UNDETECTED
    private int hiddenRead;//<--- UNDETECTED
    private int hiddenNoRead;//<--- UNDETECTED
    private int postWrite;//<--- UNDETECTED
    private int notGood;<--- found by PMD

    public static void main(String [] args)
    {
        ClassA a = new ClassA();//<--- Properly Used
        a.neverRead = 2;
        System.out.println("NW is "+neverWritten);
        ClassB b = new ClassB();//<--- Properly Used
        b.Use(hiddenRead, hiddenNoRead, postWrite);
        postWrite = 4;
        notGood++;
        ClassA a2 = new ClassA();//<--- found by PMD
    }
}
```

Figure 1: Program demonstrating expanded definition of use

trol structure of the program. The resulting conservative classification of state variables can be used to determine if one of these degenerate forms exists.

The second metric expands upon the definition of "use" in order to capture more completely the usage that can be attributed to the members of a class. Wagner et al [10] indicated that current tools such as PMD are highly accurate in identifying unused variables. Yet, in a simple experiment—shown in Figure 1—this expanded definition of "use" created by the author was used to detect 80 percent more unused variables than PMD. This expanded definition will identify variables and methods that have no semantic value in the program and "can be ignored while still producing optimal behavior." [5]

The third metric relies on a modified form of the module detection algorithm described by Blondel [1]. In the modified form, the algorithm is capable of identifying optimal module membership based on member-to-member access in the code. This allows the metric to identify probable package membership without any a priori knowledge or human interaction. The contrast between the suggested and current package structure may be used to identify inconsistencies in the design. The fact that this algorithm can be applied to class or package membership means it can also identify candidate encapsulation concerns.

The remaining metrics apply principles of graph theory to examine the source code and determine if other inconsistencies exist. Is some public variable, for example, accessed by other classes or should it be reclassified as private? Are two classes demonstrating feature envy by their strong affiliation? Are there any portions of the source code that are reachable but have no side effects? By using the three metrics above to inform this graphical analysis, it should be possible to identify several degenerate forms and bring them to the developer's attention for further analysis.

4.1 Expected Results

The selected metrics focus on principles of object-oriented software and were developed exclusively for detecting degenerate forms in OO. As such, they are of limited value as metrics, but they will make it possible to meet some basic proof of concept objectives that include:

- Evaluation in terms of false negative and positive rate,
- Validation in terms of diagnostic utility to developers,
- Development of simple automated repair functions,
- Demonstration of layers of degenerate forms, and
- Examination of abandoned software, long revision histories, and software currently under development.

In addition, the development of these metrics will allow for more extensive future experiments and tool development based on the principles learned. Refactoring may be performed in a more cost-effective manner. Development paradigms, tools, and programming practices can be examined for their efficiency in preventing the development of degenerate forms. New metrics may also be developed to identify degenerate forms that affect other programming paradigms including procedural and multi-core. As new metrics and degenerate forms are identified, the relationship between them can also be studied.

5. Evaluation Methodology

The primary outcome from this research will be the set of automated metrics and repair functions. These will be developed by testing on a large sample large-SLOC count, open source military, commercial and academic programs written in C# and Java. The sample will provide sufficient source code for baseline development as well as evaluation of the metrics. Once the metrics have been perfected, they will be individually assessed for correctness by contrasting the automated results with an expert classification by a jury. The jury will be given a random selection of classes from the source code sample and asked to determine specific characteristics related to the metrics and specific degenerate forms. The results from the jury will be used to quantify type I and type II errors for each metric.

In addition, the metrics will be tested on "live" code that is currently under development. The automated findings will be assessed by the software development team based on the degree of accuracy and the perceived value to the developers. The identification of hitherto unknown but correctly identified degenerate forms would rate high. Incorrectly identified or low-value items would rate low. These automated findings may also identify areas of degraded quality of which the developers are already aware. The results from this experiment will mirror [10] and [8] in demonstrating the value of the automated tools and the willingness of the developers to rely on those findings.

Secondarily, this research may afford future developers the ability to characterize degeneration as it occurs. Based on the work of [4], [3], and others, there are a number of causative and contributing factors that appear to lead to software degeneration. While a full study is infeasible, the validation of any of these factors would be a step in the right direction. Studies of these characteristics will assume the metrics, individually evaluated as described above, are correct and will rely on their findings to characterize the degeneration found in a sample source code. Thereafter, the selection of the source code for these contributing factors will help to prove correlation.

6. Conclusions

The proposed dissertation research will develop metrics capable of detecting degenerate forms in software. These metrics will be a first sample set to prove the value of such targeted metrics in diagnosing degenerate forms. With the addition of more metrics, it will be possible to more fully detect the extent and limits of degenerate forms. Improved detection may be used as an enabling technology to add visible, quantifiable, objective software quality metrics to development. As a result, it will be possible to:

- Overcome the sample size and other logistical concerns to enable more research on this topic,
- Conduct consistent quality assessment studies of any large-scale software project with minimal human effort,
- Identify causative or contributory factors that lead to greater risk of software degeneration, and
- Perform targeted refactoring of degenerate forms with limited knowledge of the software.

Acknowledgments

The author gratefully acknowledges the U.S. Navy for its support, the NSWCDD Software Developers' Lecture Series and Community of Practice, and his dissertation committee for its assistance. The author also lovingly acknowledges the patience of his wife and children.

References

[1] Blondel, V. D., Guillaume, J. L., Lambiotte, R., & Lefebvre, E. (2008). Fast unfolding of communities in large networks. *J. of Statistical Mechanics: Theory and Experiment, 2008*(10), P10008.

[2] Bourquin, Fabrice, and Rudolf K. Keller. "High impact refactoring based on architecture violations." *Software Maintenance and Reengineering, 2007 CSMR '07. 11th European Conference* on. IEEE, 2007.

[3] Dvorak, J. (1994). Conceptual entropy and its effect on class hierarchies. *Computer, 27*(6), 59–63.

[4] Eick, S. G., Graves, T. L., Karr, A. F., Marron, J. S., & Mockus, A. (2001). Does code decay? assessing the evidence from change management data. *Software Engineering, IEEE Transactions on, 27*(1), 1-12.

[5] Jong, N. K., & Stone, P. (2004). Towards learning to ignore irrelevant state variables. In *The AAAI-2004 Workshop on Learning and Planning in Markov Processes–Advances and Challenges.*

[6] Kemerer, C. F., & Slaughter, S. (1999). An empirical approach to studying software evolution. *Software Engineering, IEEE Transactions on, 25*(4), 493–509.

[7] Lehman, M. M., Perry, D. E., & Ramil, J. F. (1998, November). Implications of evolution metrics on software maintenance. In *Software Maintenance, 1998. Proceedings, Inter. Conf. on* (pp. 208–217). IEEE.

[8] Murphy-Hill, E., Parnin, C., & Black, A. P. (2012). How we refactor, and how we know it. *Software Engineering, IEEE Transactions on, 38*(1), 5–18.

[9] Van Gurp, J., & Bosch, J. (2002). Design erosion: problems and causes. *J. of Systems and Software, 61*(2), 105–119.

[10] Wagner, S., Jürjens, J., Koller, C., & Trischberger, P. (2005). Comparing bug finding tools with reviews and tests. In *Testing of Communicating Systems* (pp. 40–55). Springer Berlin Heidelberg.

Structured Source Retrieval for Improving Software Search during Program Comprehension Tasks

Brian Eddy

Department of Computer Science
The University of Alabama
bpeddy@crimson.ua.edu

Abstract

During the software maintenance and evolution phase, the majority of a developer's time is spent on programming comprehension tasks. Feature location (i.e., finding the first location to make a modification), impact analysis (i.e., determining what and to what extent a program is affected by a change), and traceability (i.e., determining where requirements are implemented in the program), are all examples of such tasks. Recent research in the area of program comprehension has focused on using textual information, structural information (i.e., information regarding the creation and use of objects and methods within the code), and execution traces to develop tools that ease the burden on developers and decrease the time spent in each task. Furthermore, new studies in automating these tasks have started using text retrieval techniques, such as the vector space model (VSM), latent semantic indexing (LSI), and latent Dirichlet allocation (LDA) for searching software. This doctoral symposium summary presents two promising areas for improving existing techniques by combining structural information with text retrieval. The first is a methodology for evaluating the usefulness of text obtained from a program by looking at the structural location of terms (e.g., method name, comments, identifiers). The second focuses on improving the existing text retrieval approaches by providing more flexible queries (i.e., search strings). These two areas are complementary to each other and may be combined.

1. Motivation for Structured Source Retrieval

Understanding a software system's implementation is a crucial part of a developer's job. When developers are tasked with changing the source code of a large or unfamiliar system, they must spend considerable time and effort on program comprehension activities to gain the knowledge needed to implement, correct, and complete changes. Before any changes can be made, bugs fixed, or features added, the developer must first understand the system's implementation and locate source code elements specific to the current task.

Software maintenance and evolution accounts for 60-80% [1, 5] of the cost and effort during the software life cycle, and during this time, over half [8] of developer effort is taken up in trying to understand the software system. One common task involves locating a source code element that is required for a change or modification. This process, known as feature location, becomes impractical to perform manually as the scale of modern software systems increases. Existing search tools such as keyword searches and regular expressions are limited as such techniques do not allow for searching of synonyms (missing relevant results) or searching for only a single meaning of a term when a term has multiple meanings (resulting in irrelevant results) [4]. Given these problems and the increasing size and complexity of software systems, the need for more advanced tools to aid in program comprehension is evident.

Thus, techniques and tools that can reduce the effort required for these tasks are key to minimizing software costs. Many recent studies into semi-automated techniques for program comprehension tasks are based on text retrieval (TR) methods that focus on producing corpora of text extracted from source code and performing searches over the newly created model. Common TR-based tools in the literature incorporate models such as latent semantic indexing (LSI) [4] and latent Dirichlet allocation (LDA) [3].

Previous research into TR-based techniques have attempted to combine textual information with multiple sources of structural (e.g., dependency graphs) and dynamic information (e.g., execution traces). By combining textual information with structural information and dynamic information, researchers have found an improvement over using textual information alone for some systems [10–13]. There are two existing problems with this research area. First, the research has focused on latent semantic indexing (LSI) and the vector space model (VSM), discussed in more detail later. However, more sophisticated techniques such as latent Dirichlet allocation (LDA) and other topic-modeling techniques (e.g., probabilistic LSI, Pachinko allocation, associative clustering) have been shown to produce useful results in other domains along with program comprehension tasks. Second, there has not been much investigation into the importance of each structural component (e.g., whether method calls are as important as method names).

The goal of the research presented in this doctoral symposium summary is to investigate how new structural weighting schemes (i.e., schemes that give varying weights to different structural components) affects the results of text retrieval as it applies to software maintenance tasks. The research plan will study two different techniques. The first combines structural weighting with LDA as an ad-hoc preprocessing step. The second integrates structural weighting directly into a structured text retrieval approach based on language modeling. We believe this work will lead to more relevant results and as discussed in Section 3.2, lead to a more flexible retrieval process for the developer.

SPLASH '14,   Oct 20-24 2014, Portland, OR, USA.
Copyright © 2014 ACM 978-1-4503-3208-8/14/10. . . $15.00.
http://dx.doi.org/10.1145/2660252.2660253

2. Problems of Interest

We are currently working on studying the effects of structural weighting schemes on LDA and finishing the development of tool support for the structured source retrieval approach. The main problems are discussed in this section.

2.1 RP1: Determining the effects of structural weighting schemes on LDA.

TR models operate on corpora. A corpus is a set of documents containing all text associated with the document after it has undergone a set of text transformations (i.e., preprocessing steps). Each document in one of these corpora contains the text associated with a single source code entity, typically a method. TR techniques such as LSI and VSM have shown to have their results improved when combined with additional structural and dynamic information [7, 9, 10, 13]. We propose to investigate the effect of different weighting schemes for LDA. Term weighting is a common preprocessing step. These weighting schemes will take into account the structural location (e.g., parameter, comment, method name) of a term in source documents.

One criticism of the use of advanced topic modeling approaches on source code is that terms are more sparse than in natural language documents. For instance, the most relevant topic to a method may be the one that describes the method's behavior. However, terms for that topic may be limited to the method name and parameters and it is common for the method name to be limited to the method's signature. In such a case, placing higher importance on the terms in the method name may result in higher probability of a document being associated with the correct topic(s). However, this does not necessarily indicate that other terms should be disregarded. Emphasizing certain terms (e.g., method names) while deemphasizing others (e.g., method calls) may lead to a better topic model.

2.2 RP2: Determining how various weighting schemes affect structured source retrieval in language models for software maintenance tasks.

RP1 focuses on a traditional TR technique (LDA). Traditional techniques treat documents as unordered collections of terms without structure. However, not all documents are unstructured. For instance, a scientific article may be broken into the title, the abstract, the sections, the paragraphs, and the sentences. Words may appear in multiple components of the document or in a single component of the document. The approach of performing information retrieval by breaking documents into fragments based on the structure of the document, and either returning the most relevant fragments as a result of a query or using the fragments to find the most relevant documents, is known as structured document retrieval [6]. The structure of a document may be either explicitly defined using a mark-up language (e.g., XML) or derived.

We have investigated an approach to structured document retrieval on source code by deriving structure from the position and origin of the terms (e.g. method signature, method body, comments). Structured source retrieval techniques allow for new querying methodologies. For instance, a developer may have an understanding of what terms relate to method names and class names, and what terms refer to variables or fields. A developer might also have expectations of what context a term is used. Allowing a more robust query system that allows developer input may increase the likelihood of returning relevant results. Current queries used in software search do not allow for order of terms or for varying levels of emphasis on different structural components.

We will first finish a study of the benefits and consequences of the structured source retrieval technique and then investigate the combination of structured source retrieval with structural weighting from RP1.

3. The Approach

In this section, we describe the approach to structural weighting as well as our approach to structured document retrieval. We will first study the effects of structural weighting on LDA, then develop the tools needed for the structured document retrieval approach and study the effects of structural weighting on that technique. Once both parts are completed, we will compare the results of both approaches.

3.1 Structural Weighting

Structural weighting was introduced for LDA by Bassett and Kraft [2]. In their study, they focused on various weighting schemes of method names and method calls by changing term counts during the creation of the corpus. They found that by changing the count of certain terms, it was possible to achieve more accurate results with LDA.

There is still work to be completed on this idea. We will expand upon the previous research by focusing on other terms that will likely lead to an overall improvement in relevant results. There are a number of different structural components at both the method and the class level. Prior research has focused mainly on the method level for text retrieval tasks. At the method level, different weights can be placed on the following components: parameters, string literals, local variables, method calls, annotations, class or interface references, method names, in-line comments, block comments. Each of these components may be weighted individually or as a group with other items on the list. Previous experience has shown that there are two things that need to be considered: the individual component alone and the interaction between components.

A document in LDA is a collection of terms appearing in that document. Weights will be introduced to LDA through the use of scalar multiples that increase or decrease the number of times certain terms appear in these collections. A weighting scheme is then expressed as the scalar multiple for each component. By using scalar multiples and weighting the components differently, LDA may be modified to increase the probablity that certain terms will be associated with a particular document. We believe certain elements are more important to a method. For instance, method names are more important than method calls as they describe the behavior of the method itself, while a method call may be to a supporting object such as a logger or only a sub step of the method's behavior. By raising the weights on these terms we emphasize what we believe to be important, while deemphasizing what we believe to be unimportant. This produces results where methods with terms appearing in the method names are places higher than methods with terms appearing in the method calls.

Investigating this idea will start by focusing on a small subset of the components that are believed to have a high likelihood to influence the results. The initial focus will be on the leading comments, method names, parameters, and body comments. It is believed that leading comments are often used to explain the purpose of the method in natural language and therefore have a high relevance to the software search. Parameters are the inputs to the functions. Combined with the method name, they help to clarify the main responsibility of the method or help clarify which method is most relevant to a query amongst a set of overloaded methods. We will study these components by first identifying appropriate levels for the scalars applied to each component, then systematically changing the weights of each of these terms individually and as linear combinations, then performing feature location on multiple open source software systems (jEdit, JabRef, Eclipse). We will use statistical analysis to identify significance of an effective change and to identify interactions among the components.

3.2 Structured Source Retrieval

Structural Weighting offers the possibility of improvement in traditional TR-based techniques. However, structured source retrieval differs from traditional techniques by building structured documents from source code.

Structured document retrieval divides the terms in a document into multiple components where each component is a structural field of the document. For instance, a document could be divided into the title and the body of the document. For source code where documents are typically methods in the software system, the document could be divided in multiple different ways. One method could split the method signature, method body, and comments into different components. Another might only use the method signature and method body. Yet, another might split the method signature, method identifiers, method literals, and method comments. While there are several ways to perform this splitting, a finer granularity leads to more flexibility when querying but also leads to more complexity in the retrieval model. Research will need to be done to determine the best way of forming structured method documents.

Once the source code has been converted into structured documents, tools exist for indexing such documents. Indri[1] is a search engine developed as part of the Lemur project between the University of Massachusetts and Carnegie Mellon University. The search engine supports structured query documents and provides the user of the system with a flexible model for defining fields and other attributes of a document in the corpus. The system uses a combination of language modeling and inference networks as the search engine's retrieval model. We will adapt our source code model to be searchable by Indri's search engine.

The Indri query language allows for a wide variety of options. The simplest queries in Indri take the form:

#combine(side1 computes Point)

The # signifies a query, *combine* means to search for the terms together in a document, while the query is provided in the parentheses. For such a query, each term in the query is given equal weighting and the query is issued across all fields. This query does not make use of the structured document, but instead uses the document as a collection of words similar to the traditional TR approaches. A more advanced query would be of the form:

#weight(2.0 #combine[signature](area) 1.0
#combine[body](area))

In the example query, the developer has given greater weight to documents with "area" appearing in the method signature versus the method body. Perhaps the developer knows the method they want computes an area, so they believe that "area" is likely to be in the method name. They want to see methods with "area" in the method name before other possible choices. In the example given, area has twice the effect on the final score when it appears in the signature compared to the body. If we treat b as the belief score (i.e., how likely we believe the document will return this word) then an example of the overall score for a document given the example query might be $0.67 * log(b(\#combine[signature](area))) + 0.33 * log(b(\#combine[body](area)))$.

By weighting the query, developers are more likely to retrieve the results they want. While developers may manually weight their queries, we also wish to identify queries that may return higher results for developers that are less familiar with the system or suggest queries that may produce more relevant results to the developer. The focus of this research is on using the weighted queries to produce more relevant results.

4. Evaluation Methodology

To evaluate our structural weighting schemes and our structured source retrieval approach, we will use established benchmarks in the field of feature location. We will begin by repeating the study conducted by Bassett and Kraft [2]. Then we will expand our study to look at terms from the method signature, the leading comments, and body comments. We believe these components are the most likely to lead to more relevant results. We will perform statistical testing to look for significant effects between different weighting schemes and factor analysis to identify any interactions.

Once we have completed our work on LDA, we will finish development of the tools needed for our structured document retrieval technique. We will use a methodology similar to that of studying structural weighting on LDA to study the effects of different weighted queries. We will then compare the results of the two different approaches (structural weighting with LDA and structured source retrieval). Finally, we will assess whether either of these techniques results in an improvement over traditional TR-based techniques on impact analysis.

References

[1] G. Alkhatib. The maintenance problem of application software: an empirical analysis. *Journal of Software Maintenance: Research and Practice*, 4(2):83–104, 1992.

[2] B. Bassett and N. A. Kraft. Structural information based term weighting in text retrieval for feature location. In *Program Comprehension (ICPC), 2013 IEEE 21st International Conference on*, pages 133–141. IEEE, 2013.

[3] D. Blei, A. Ng, and M. Jordan. Latent Dirichlet allocation. *Journal of Machine Learning Research*, 3:993–1022, 2003.

[4] S. Deerwester, S. Dumais, G. Furnas, T. Landauer, and R. Harshman. Indexing by latent semantic analysis. *Journal of the American Society of Information Science*, 41:391–407, 1990.

[5] L. Erlikh. Leveraging legacy system dollars for e-business. *IEEE IT Pro*, pages 17–23, May/June 2000.

[6] M. Lalmas and R. Baeza-Yates. *Structured Document Retrieval*. Springer US, 2009.

[7] D. Liu, A. Marcus, D. Poshyvanyk, and V. Rajlich. Feature location via information retrieval based filtering of a single scenario execution trace. In *Proceedings of the 22nd International Conference on Automated Software Engineering*, pages 234–243, 2007.

[8] H. Müller, J. Jahnke, D. Smith, M.-A. Storey, S. Tilley, and K. Wong. Reverse engineering: A roadmap. In *Proceedings of the Future of Software Engineering*, pages 47–60, June 2000.

[9] D. Poshyvanyk, Y. Gueheneuc, A. Marcus, G. Antoniol, and V. Rajlich. Feature location using probabilistic ranking of methods based on execution scenarios and information retrieval. *IEEE Transactions on Software Engineering*, 33(6):420–432, June 2007.

[10] M. Revelle, B. Dit, and D. Poshyvanyk. Using data fusion and web mining to support feature location in software. In *Proceedings of 18th IEEE International Conference on Program Comprehension*, pages 14–23, Braga, Portugal, July 2010.

[11] G. Scanniello and A. Marcus. Clustering support for static concept location in source code. In *Proceedings of the 19th IEEE International Conference on Program Comprehension*, 2011.

[12] P. Shao and R. K. Smith. Feature location by ir modules and call graph. In *Proceedings of the 47th Annual Southeast Regional Conference*, pages 70:1–70:4, Clemson, South Carolina, 2009. ISBN 978-1-60558-421-8.

[13] W. Zhao, L. Zhang, Y. Liu, J. Sun, and F. Yang. SNIAFL: Towards a static noninteractive approach to feature location. *ACM Transactions of Software Engineering Methodologies*, 15(2):195–226, 2006.

---

[1] http://www.lemurproject.org/indri/

High-Performance Language Interoperability in Multi-Language Runtimes

Matthias Grimmer

Johannes Kepler University, Linz
grimmer@ssw.jku.at

Abstract

Programs often consist of parts that are written in different languages because sub-problems lend themselves to being implemented in a particular language. However, multi-language programs often suffer from poor performance, complex cross-language interfaces, or insufficient flexibility. We propose a novel approach for composing multiple language implementations in a seamless way. Foreign objects of one language can be used like regular objects in another language. Our interoperability mechanism targets language implementations that run on the same VM and have the same style of intermediate representation (IR), e.g., an abstract syntax tree (AST). For accessing foreign objects we generate foreign-language-specific IR patterns that we insert into the IR of the host application. Thus we avoid converting or marshalling foreign objects at the language border. Our mechanism also allows the just-in-time compiler of the host VM to inline and optimize across language borders.

Categories and Subject Descriptors D.3.4 [*Programming Languages*]: Processors—Run-time environments, Code generation, Interpreters, Compilers, Optimization

Keywords cross-language; language interoperability; virtual machine; optimization; language implementation

1. Motivation

Large software projects often mix multiple programming languages because this allows developers to express each part of a problem in the most suitable language. These parts are connected by a cross-language interface that provides infrastructure for invoking methods or functions from other languages and for exchanging data.

SPLASH '14, Oct 20–24, 2014, Portland, OR, USA.
Copyright is held by the owner/author(s).
ACM 978-1-4503-3208-8/14/10.
http://dx.doi.org/10.1145/2660252.2660256

However, language interoperability is hard because different languages use a wide spectrum of paradigms and features, such as: object-oriented versus non-object oriented; array-based versus non-array-based; dynamically typed versus statically typed; explicit memory management versus automatic memory management.

We present our idea of a cross-language mechanism that makes these differences completely transparent by allowing programmers to directly pass objects from one language to another. Our goal is to use foreign objects like regular objects in the host language and to hide the different language paradigms. For example, consider the JavaScript statement in Figure 1:

```
local = obj.value + ...
```

Figure 1: Using foreign objects transparently.

If `obj` were a C structure or a Ruby object (i.e., a *foreign object*), the statement should still be able to access its `value` property as if it were the property of a JavaScript object. Also, our project aims at removing performance barriers between languages and supporting their interoperability even if the languages use different programming paradigms.

In this paper we call every entity of a program an *object*, e.g., JavaScript objects, C pointers, as well as functions or methods. Object accesses are operations that can be performed on objects, e.g., method calls or property accesses.

2. Problem

We focus our work on an interoperability mechanism that targets language implementations, hosted by a general-purpose VM. In the context of this paper, a *language implementation* translates the source code of an application into an intermediate representation (IR) and executes it on the underlying VM (e.g. the Java Virtual Machine [1]). To achieve our vision of transparent language interoperability we have to answer the following research questions:

(1) How can we build a flexible cross-language mechanism that allows us to transparently use foreign objects? To interface arbitrary languages without additional glue code

we make objects *sharable* so that different language implementations can access them.

(2) How can languages with different object models avoid marshalling and conversion at the language borders? We aim to avoid the conversion of objects when they cross language boundaries, but allow every language to have its own object model. Finally, a foreign object access has to be transparent to the just-in-time (JIT) compiler and it should be able to optimize the foreign object access like a regular object access.

2.1 State of the Art

Language interoperability is a well-researched area: The Microsoft Common Language Infrastructure (CLI) describes language implementations that compile different languages to a common IR that is executed by a common runtime [5]. The CLI describes a Common Language Specification (CLS) for cross-language interoperability. It defines a common object model, a fixed set of data types, and operations that all language implementations have to use. However, this approach restricts the flexibility of CLS-compliant languages. Our goal is to allow every language to have its own object model, which other languages can access.

Another common solution is using an Interface Description Language (IDL). An IDL describes the interface of a software component that is written in a foreign language. The IDL interface is translated to stubs in the host and target language, which can then be used for cross-language communication [2]. These stubs marshal data to and from a common wire representation. The drawbacks of this approach include performance overhead because of marshaling, programming effort and inflexibility. We strive for an approach that allows to transparently use foreign objects without needing any boilerplate code.

Wegiel and Krintz [7] propose a language-neutral object model that bridges different programming languages running on different runtime systems. Different VMs can share objects via a separate heap. However, programming languages fundamentally differ in their paradigms (e.g. JavaScript's dynamic objects versus structures in C), which makes a language-neutral object model hardly applicable. Instead, objects should be shared between languages directly.

A lot of other work explicitly addresses a fixed pair of languages [3, 6, 8]. These approaches are tailored towards interoperability between two specific languages and cannot be generalized for arbitrary languages and VMs.

3. Approach

Truffle [9] is a platform for building high-performance language implementations. A language implementation hosted by Truffle is expressed as an AST interpreter. The Truffle ASTs are evaluated by recursive execution of `execute` methods defined in every node class. We use Truffle and its

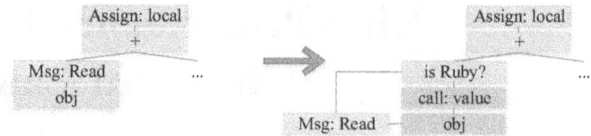

Figure 2: Message Resolution; JavaScript AST of Figure 1 using a Ruby object.

guest languages (JavaScript, Ruby, R and C) as the basis of our cross-language mechanism:

Although syntactic differences are abstracted away by compiling different languages to an AST, each language uses its own representation of objects. In order to answer our research question (1) and to make objects *sharable* across different languages, we require them to support a common interface, which is a set of *messages*, such as *read*, *write*, or *call*. We then replace every language-specific object access with a language-independent message so that all interactions between a program and its objects happen via messages. This allows us to generalize the AST of an application and to make object accesses language independent.

3.1 Message Resolution

The receiver of a message does not return a *value* that can be further processed, but rather an *AST snippet* that contains receiver-language specific operations for executing the message on the receiver object. We replace the AST part that sent the message with the returned snippet (*message resolution*). For example, we replace the AST of a language-independent *Read* message with receiver-language-specific operations that directly read a property from the receiver (see Figure 2). Subsequent executions of this object access now directly access the object rather than sending a message. If the foreign receiver does not support a message, it will not resolve it, which means that the object access is not possible. Creating interoperability code at runtime in the course of message resolution combines flexibility with high performance, which answers our research question (2).

A foreign object might be replaced with some other foreign object at run time originating from a different language. Hence we check the receiver's language of origin. If the receiver is a foreign object of a different language than the one seen so far, we again send a message to it. We call object accesses with different receiver-languages *language-polymorphic*. A language polymorphic access is resolved into language-specific AST patterns that are embedded into the AST like an inline cache [4].

3.2 Shared Primitive Values

To exchange primitive values we use a set of *shared primitive values*. Two languages exchange primitive values by mapping their primitive values to these values. However, if a language cannot map a primitive value onto a *shared primitive value*, it has to be exchanged as a non-primitive foreign object and is accessed via messages. Such non-primitive objects can cause run-time type errors, e.g., when operations expect a primitive value. However, this guarantees that conversions are safe and no information is lost.

This approach works well in practice: For example, Ruby values of type *Float*, JavaScript values of type *Number*, elements of an R *double precision* vector, or C values of type *double* are all mapped to a *floating point primitive* and are therefore compatible.

3.3 Performance

The idea of message resolution is to replace a language-independent message with an AST pattern that performs a language-specific access, which only affects the application performance at the first execution of an object access. After that the application runs at full speed and foreign object accesses do not cause an overhead in peak performance.

Since language implementations on top of Truffle generally lead to high-performance code [9], we also expect multi-language applications to perform well. The Truffle framework starts interpreting the AST, possibly produced by different language implementations. When the execution frequency of an AST exceeds a predefined threshold the JIT compiler translates it to machine code. By generating AST patterns for accessing foreign objects we create a single homogeneous AST unit and thus avoid compilation barriers that would otherwise prevent optimizations such as inlining. If a JIT compiler optimizes this unit, any language-specific parts are completely transparent, which allows the compiler to inline method calls even if the receiver is a foreign object. Widening the compilation span across different languages enables the compiler to apply optimizations to a wider range of code.

4. Evaluation Methodology

To evaluate our technique we are following an iterative approach: Our first step was to approve the hypothesis of providing a seamless way that allows combining different languages without writing boilerplate code (corresponding to research question (1)). Therefore we implemented our interface for the Truffle guest languages JavaScript, Ruby, R, and C. Given these language implementations we can already show that our approach is applicable for multi-language applications that consist of these four languages.

Finally, we want to demonstrate that our approach is of relevance for existing real-world scenarios. We will use our mechanism and compose the Ruby and C implementation on top of Truffle and support the C extension API for Ruby. Our goal is to run real-world Ruby applications that make heavy use of C extensions and show that our novel approach performs well compared to existing solutions.

Our strongest hypothesis (corresponding to research question (2)) claims that a foreign object access does not cause any overhead in peak performance because of message

resolution. Our current prototype allows us to evaluate the mechanism on handcrafted microbenchmarks, which back our claim. By using representative multi-language benchmarks we will show that foreign object accesses do not cause any overhead in peak performance.

5. Conclusion

This paper presented our ongoing research to achieve high-performance interoperability between programming languages hosted by a common VM. We allow programmers to use foreign objects as if they were regular objects and make the language boundary completely opaque. We introduce a message interface for sharable objects, which allows different language implementations to exchange objects. Language implementations access shared objects via object- and language-independent messages. Our resolving approach transforms these messages to an object- and language-specific accesses at runtime. The mechanism therefore refrains from converting objects. Instead, we adapt the AST of a program to deal with the foreign objects. Message resolution allows us to combine language implementations without affecting the peak performance of the individual implementations. The resolved AST of a program completely obliterates the language boundaries, which enables a JIT compiler to perform its optimizations even across language borders.

References

[1] HotSpot JVM. Java version history (J2SE 1.3). http://en.wikipedia.org/wiki/Java_version_history, 2013.

[2] Common Object Request Brooker Architecture (CORBA) Specification. http://www.omg.org/spec/CORBA/3.3/, 2014.

[3] K. E. Gray, R. Findler, and M. Flatt. Fine-grained interoperability through mirrors and contracts. pages 231–245, 2005.

[4] U. Hölzle, C. Chambers, and D. Ungar. Optimizing dynamically-typed object-oriented languages with polymorphic inline caches. Lecture Notes in Computer Science, pages 21–38. Springer Berlin Heidelberg, 1991. ISBN 978-3-540-54262-9. .

[5] E. Meijer and J. Gough. Technical overview of the common language runtime. *language*, 29:7, 2001.

[6] J. Rose and H. Muller. Integrating the Scheme and C languages. In *Proceedings of the 1992 ACM conference on Lisp and functional programming*, pages 247–259. ACM, 1992.

[7] M. Wegiel and C. Krintz. Cross-language, type-safe, and transparent object sharing for co-located managed runtimes.

[8] T. Wrigstad, F. Z. Nardelli, S. Lebresne, J. Östlund, and J. Vitek. Integrating typed and untyped code in a scripting language. POPL '10, pages 377–388, New York, NY, USA, 2010. ACM. ISBN 978-1-60558-479-9.

[9] T. Würthinger, C. Wimmer, A. Wöß, L. Stadler, G. Duboscq, C. Humer, G. Richards, D. Simon, and M. Wolczko. One VM to rule them all. In *Proceedings of the 2013 ACM international symposium on New ideas, new paradigms, and reflections on programming & software*, pages 187–204. ACM, 2013.

HCI Metacomputing

Universal Syntax, Structured Editing, and Deconstructible User Interfaces

Christopher Hall

University of California, Santa Barbara
chall01@cs.ucsb.edu

Abstract

There is a classic design tension between user-friendly user interface design and expert-friendly user interface design. There is also a classic design tension between binary data format design and printable data format design. This work attempts to expose both sets of design tensions as having the same cause and solution. We observe an opportunity to redefine the baseline for "human-readable" formats by pairing a universal binary syntax with a universal structured editor and explore the rippling implications that it could have on human-computer interaction and the computing landscape at large. We discuss how this paradigm solves a host of typical bugs and developer pain points as well as making software more flexible, how it can be used to add a self-descriptive capacity to information representations ranging from data formats to user interfaces, and finally, how that creates new outlets for end-users to apply tiers of computational literacy for their own empowerment.

Categories and Subject Descriptors   D.2.6 [*Programming Environments*]: Interactive environments; E.2 [*Data Storage Representations*]: Object representation; I.7.2 [*Document/Text Processing*]: hypermedia, markup languages; K.3.2 [*Computing Milieux*]: Literacy

Keywords   data metaformat; abstract syntax tree; metadata; structured editing; user interface architecture; usability metadesign

1. Motivation

In software engineering literature, modifiability and maintainability are valued, but surveys across usability considerations [1] turn up no attributes resembling what we would call 'adaptability'. This is of perpetual concern because user-interface designers cannot consider all possible use cases of their systems and predict the evolving needs of their users. Worse yet, they often have to leave functionality unexposed due to various design considerations ranging from beginner friendliness to aesthetics. For instance, not all lists in applications can be exported, sorted, searched, or otherwise processed at the users desire unless the developer explicitly offers those individual features. The degree of a user's computational literacy does not earn them proportional utility or control over their applications. Acts of using and writing software are unnecessarily segregated by differing architectural paradigms. Thus, there is no incentive to invest in incremental literacy, nor an *in-situ* way to explore it.

User interfaces are the means to perceive and manipulate application models, acting essentially as special-cased structured editors, guiding interactions through syntactically or semantically valid workflows. Since software is intangible and only has the face given to it by the user interface design, there is nothing 'under the surface' to provide human intelligibility to the more general underlying runtime models. Unlike with physical artifacts like automobile engines or origami creations, having a running piece of software in front of you is not by nature also a means to view, learn from, and adapt its design to capture unforeseen opportunities and parameters. This has created a curious mutual exclusion between transparency and user interfaces. Domain-tailored user interfaces present data in a structured but rigid and opaque way. For example, if the text is too long for the user interface label to display in the given layout, the text is truncated often with no way to obtain the full original text. At the other extreme, when developers work with formal languages they use "human-readable" lexical syntax, painstakingly manipulating data on an overly granular character level. Nearly all human interactions take place at one of these two extremes, either undermining the flexibility of digital tools, or requiring complexity to continuously reparse flat delicate sequences. Representative ramifications of this include: Different sets of characters are off limits in various types of content; file names cannot contain /:*?; domain names, hashtags, and identifiers cannot contain spaces; etc. When sorting strings or filenames, "Track10" comes before

SPLASH '14,   Oct 20-24, 2014, Portland, OR, USA.
Copyright © 2014 ACM 978-1-4503-3208-8/14/10. . . $15.00.
http://dx.doi.org/10.1145/2660252.2660258

"Track9" in lexicographical order. Repeated substrings are also repeated in the byte buffer, wasting memory and requiring that changes to those strings be repeated for each. Two programmers looking at the same copy of source code cannot be each seeing it formatted to their unique needs and preferences.

2. Problem

We trace these high-level modularity, flexibility, and HCI problems to low level fundamentals of interoperation, metadata capacity, and human-readability. Since Unix, "the structure of files is controlled by the programs that use them, not by the system"[4]. This was a critical step for the flexibility of software, yet left information representations with no common ground to appreciate each other's structures without also having to understand their semantics. User interfaces, runtimes, and data formats alike are left to provide their own means to bootstrap structure from raw bits. For this discussion, we organize the space of possible schemes into two major paradigms which we dub qualitative and quantitative syntax.

2.1 Qualitative Syntax

Most anything textual is this paradigm, including source code. It consists of using predesignated symbols/tokens (a finite lexicon) reserved to represent both structure and type control signals. Though especially familiar to programmers, we summarize it here to highlight it as having drawbacks in relation to an alternative.

In qualitative syntax, units of structure extend *until* encountering a symbol designated as its terminator. e.g. A sentence continues until a period, a C string continues until a null byte, a file in DOS continues until character 26 (EOF). In many cases a token continues until a value that is not in an alphabet for that type. In order to nest hierarchies of data, a different token is used to distinguish each end. e.g. In C-based languages, code blocks deepen with '{' and shallow with '}'. Comment blocks use '/*' and '*/' but sadly do not nest. The nature of context specific delimiters cause local lexical analysis to be married to overarching grammar.

The choices of control symbols are technically arbitrary, but whatever they are, they can not be used as content values without further signals reserved to mean that the next unit is to be taken as literal. Embedding one encoding within another requires padding with these 'escape sequences' wherever it collides with the context's control values. This is ugly, hard to read, discourages layered architecture, and leads to an entire genre of bugs and security vulnerabilities requiring diligent programming and input processing. Furthermore, the size of the encoding grows at a rate exponential in the number of embeddings. e.g. When matching a \ using a regular expression written in Javascript being generated by a C program, eight slashes are needed: \\\\\\\\ (not counting quote escaping).

2.2 Quantitative Syntax

In quantitative syntax, the length quantities for units of structure are provided upfront in one form or another. In other words, the amount of addressing to skip in order to reach the end of that item. At its simplest, this directly encodes a tokenization. Here is a contrived example assuming a simple textual single-character length preamble preceding each element: 3www2w33org would encode the URL for the W3C without the need to ever have chosen a particular character to act as the domain name delimiter. Note that this keeps the structural part of syntax from being content or grammar sensitive. This paradigm has none of the drawbacks mentioned in the context of qualitative syntax, however, it requires some degree of mechanical logic to author because there are invariants that need to be upheld. If edited directly, length values in the headers must be updated to match any changes in content size. Thus, this paradigm tends not to exist outside the context of executing software.

2.3 Parsed and Unparsed Realms - We only Need One

Generally, qualitative syntax is used when communicating with users, quantitative syntax is used by runtimes. Parsers transform the former into the latter (ASTs are formed through the counting and replacement of tokens with quantities). All programming language runtimes use a mixture of fixed and dynamic width quantitative syntax for in-memory structures (though not serialized). It is also used by the more structured efficiency-conscious binary formats such as Matlab (.mat), PNG, and by runtime-centric RPC-protocol metaformats such as Protocol Buffers and Thrift.

Computing takes on the complexity of supporting both paradigms, constantly moving between parsed and unparsed forms because "the transparency and interoperability benefits of textual formats are sufficiently strong that most designers have resisted the temptation to optimize for performance at the cost of readability"[3]. The costs for this readability are even broader than sheer performance. Ironically, textual formats do not end up being all that easy to read, edit, or interoperate. Try manually rerouting to an embedded URL that has been escaped, or moving a document between MS Word and LaTeX. With the wide variety of existing lexical schemes and the fact that their formatting is baked into their content, make it cumbersome for any editor to competently collapse chosen aspects of the data out of view. This has always limited the prospects for authoring and viewing layered, multi-dimensional, or metadata-laden content in a raw form. This seems to leave no ideal options for bootstrapping transparent intuitive structure in computing.

Metaformats, e.g. XML and JSON, take advantage of the fact that syntax and semantics are separable. They offer lexical and syntactic foundations along with libraries for marshalling data. This makes it convenient to build more specific formats on their foundation. However, of the 16 metaformats we looked at, all have used a qualitative token-based syntax with the exception of those that are RPC oriented, and none of these approaches have ever simultaneously provided efficient binary encoding, recursive metadata on any element, full self-description, and human readability.

There is an opportunity to circumvent the trade off that ties freestanding data to qualitative lexical syntax and unite both ends of the spectrum based on three observations: One, *all* **formats are encoding trees** or special cases of trees. Two, we are no longer technologically constrained by purely textual typewriters and teletypes as the common denominator for input/output. Three, it is not that the bit sequences of textual format encodings like UTF8 are somehow intrinsically understandable to a human; "human readability" just colloquially implies that it is a standard encoding readable by a terminal or text editor. The sense of intrinsic readability merely comes from the ubiquity of tools that render ASCII and unicode. Technically, any format could achieve this same status if it and its editors are general purpose enough to warrant an equal ubiquity.

3. Approach

Our approach consists of two mutually supportive aspects: a self-describing binary metaformat with metadata semantics, and a graphical-syntax structured editor. The tight pairing of these concepts is critical; they allow each other to be general purpose and simultaneously amplify human and machine readability.

At the physical encoding level, units of data are preceded by a binary header comprised of a scope-length value (quantitative syntax) and a node-type value (self-description). The node type enables an editor to provide an appropriate human-intelligible representation for the encoding used by each individual fragment of data. The main design decision that needs coordinated agreement across implementations is the set of node-types to define. A minimum of three are necessary to achieve our minimum goals and upgrade flat-files to have structural transparency: a leaf type, array, and metadata. We allow ourselves only up to 16 node types in order to fit into a half-byte, and the extra 13 values can all be leveraged for dramatic efficiency opportunities to take a load off of what would otherwise fall to microformats in metadata. For example, one value is allocated to Integer and one to Floating Point (IEEE). These combine elegantly with the length field to subsume a full spectrum of bit-width varieties (8, 16, 24, 32, 40, ...).

In its most basic form, the editor can be seen as a text editor augmented with quantitative syntax support - a simple layer of indirection that visually abstracts the syntax headers in the data as pure language-agnostic structure. This liberates the metaformat to use a non-token syntax paradigm while *improving* human-readability. For illustration, see figure 1. Just as in a text editor, representations can be directly and freely edited, but retaining an abstract form of syntax. This greatly reduces clutter for concrete languages built to

take advantage of the lack of need for structural tokens, or for traditional languages that are supported by a plugin that parses them into these abstract syntax trees for better viewing and editing. A new 'structural literacy' for authoring explicit structure can then be amortized across all of computing, for user and system alike.

Figure 1. Top: bytes of a URL in hex. Blue - UTF8 and Text Editor interpretation. Green - Universal Syntax and Data Editor interpretation. Bottom: contrast in human readable form.

3.1 Metadata

Fully general metadata semantics are a critical component for extensible and composable modeling. The metadata node-type marks metadata to be associated with the node immediately previous to it in the encoding. Any tree can be added as metadata to any other recursively. This allows models to be as **self-describing** as desired. We know of no existing metaformat that supports free-form recursive metadata. Annotations themselves can be marked as owned, maintained, or intended for some application or class of applications such that they can communicate to each other indirectly via the data itself as it moves between software. It can be used to embed output on the input it is based on, or the other way around to retain the context being shed as models are transformed/compiled so that the transformations are stand-alone reversible or self-documenting.

A special node-type called 'semantic' can be placed in metadata on a node to tag it as intending to have specific meaning to the client software as opposed to it having to be recognized *a priori* as a reserve word. This bootstraps the logic layer of the metaformat in an unambiguous way that allows clients to know when they do not understand something that they should. Using this semantic node-type we can define labels and references that allow for encoding general graphs. We can also provide an extended version of Ted Nelson's transclusion[2] - a query model inlines virtual subnodes from other locations in the tree and dynamically composes, filters, substitutes, or preprocesses source material as desired. These can reduce storage size by normalizing redundant data without changing the model, or express referential identity, making refactoring operations trivial and robust. This opens the door for non-literal relationships with even raw data. The physical layer can have a different structure than the logical layer. For example, the model design can be string-based, and the encoding can automatically derive use of more efficient enumeration values under the hood. This relieves users of a major design trade-off. We believe the metaformat design is general and efficient enough to capture any data model, warranting a ubiquity rival to text editors.

3.2 Deconstructible User Interfaces

Once all data has metadata capacity, markup languages can be mixed-in to augment any data at any time with high-level types and presentation descriptions. Object-oriented agents can then be automatically attached to individual subtrees to provide various layouts, abstractions, visualizations, or interactive APIs that uphold invariants across operations. This can include enforcing a particular grammar and guiding edits toward only valid expressions. Agent implementations live on the client and take care of mapping to platform specific modalities. This paradigm is about feeding a multitude of micro applications and user interfaces to data as opposed to the other way around. These data-driven layers can themselves remain hierarchical because the metaformat/data-editor pair solve a fractal problem of structured interaction in a fractal way. They can be combined and layered recursively, maintaining the provenance of each model and view's inputs. One can imagine incrementally approximating a full-fledged traditional graphical user interface, which can then, by construction, be peeled back apart on the fly for any number of reasons. This is along the lines of a browser DOM that is more layered, persistent, directly authorable, suitable to any encoding, not tied to any one markup/computation language, does not represent just one fixed chunk of document at a time, and whose selective presentation, loading, collapse, and expansion of subsections does not rely on a designer's script.

To a developer, there is value in prototyping and testing each layer in an application's architecture incrementally. Being able to have GUIs along the way cleans up and assists every task with high-level support. Thus, there is an incentive to approach development as structural data modelling with adaptable views and APIs for each milestone, starting very general and finishing very specialized. This approach not only results in applications that are technically usable even before top level GUIs are designed for them, but also the user benefits from having a cascade of surfaces to fall back on in exceptional circumstances by no perception of additional effort on the part of the developers to provide. In fact, it may often result in less work since more of the pieces are likely to be reusable across communities. This gives applications a spreadsheet-like quality. Suitable for many gradations of end-user programming.

At its most humble, this approach scales down to represent a single classical string, with a single byte of header overhead (equivalent footprint of a null-terminated C string). At its most ambitious, it scales up to approximate full application UIs that can be, by nature, deconstructed by end users if the polished surface they have been given ever falls short of their needs. They will have "a hood to lift" and a surface to apply their computational literacy to, but always with high-level representations. This platform's killer app is to kill apps, readily absorbing the roles of calculators, spreadsheets, word processors, CLIs, IDEs, and web browsers alike, in a more fluid, granular, interoperable, and reusable way.

4. Evaluation Methodology

We will demonstrate that existing metaformats such as XML, JSON, and Protocol Buffers, as well as domain-specific formats such as BMP and PNG, can be rebuilt on top of our proposed universal syntax with improved readability, feature set, and space and time performance. We will employ user studies to compare the usability of our editor with that of classical text editors for common editing and formal language authoring tasks. We will demonstrate that a cross section of personal computing applications can be rebuilt in this paradigm with identical or equivalent user experience, while earning unprecedented adaptability, code unification, and literacy benefits. We have a backlog of wishlist application extension and UI modification case-studies to indulge as proof-of-concept for increases in end-user empowerment. We should be able to show a measured decrease in average lines of new code per application and UI development time. Ideally, we would capture evidence of users having propensity to acquire incremental computational literacy as a result of it being useful and being surrounded by architectural transparency and a continuum of live examples.

References

[1] E. Folmer, J. van Gurp, and J. Bosch. A framework for capturing the relationship between usability and software architecture. *Software Process: Improvement and Practice*, 8(2):67–87, 2003.

[2] T. H. Nelson. Xanalogical structure, needed now more than ever: parallel documents, deep links to content, deep versioning, and deep re-use. *ACM Computing Surveys (CSUR)*, 31 (4es):33, 1999.

[3] E. S. Raymond. *The art of Unix programming*. Addison-Wesley Professional, 2003.

[4] D. M. Ritchie and K. Thompson. The unix time-sharing system. *Commun. ACM*, 26(1):84–89, Jan. 1983. ISSN 0001-0782. .

An Approach to Safely Evolve Program Families in C

Flávio Medeiros

Federal University of Campina Grande (UFCG), Campina Grande, PB, Brazil
flaviomedeiros@copin.ufcg.edu.br

Abstract

The C preprocessor is widely used to handle variability and solve portability issues in program families. In this context, developers normally use tools like *GCC* and *Clang*. However, these tools are not variability-aware, i.e., they preprocess the code and consider each family member individually. As a result, even well-known and widely used families, such as *Linux* and *Apache*, contain bad smells and bugs related to variability. To minimize this problem, we propose an approach to safely evolve C program families. We develop a strategy to detect bugs related to variability and define refactorings to remove bad smells in preprocessor directives. Our supporting tool, *Colligens*, implements our strategy to detect bugs and applies our refactorings automatically. By using our approach in 40 program families, we detect 121 bugs related to variability, and developers accepted 78% of the patches we submit. Also, we remove 477 bad smells in 12 C program families without clone code as in previous studies.

Categories and Subject Descriptors D.2.3 [*Software Engineering*]: Coding Tools and Techniques

Keywords Program Families; Preprocessors; Bugs; Bad Smells; Refactorings

1. Motivation

Developers often use C to develop infrastructure software like web servers, such as *Apache* and *Cherokee*, and operating systems such as *Linux* and *Android*. Infrastructure software requires variability to run on different platforms. In this context, developers normally use preprocessors to handle variability and portability problems [2]. By using the C preprocessor, developers encompass parts of the source code with preprocessor directives, such as `#ifdef` and `#endif`. In other words, developers deal with a family of programs, which is a set of similar programs whose commonality is so extensive that it is useful to study their common properties before analyzing individual family members [8].

Program families implementing multi-platform infrastructure software, e.g., *Apache* and *Linux*, evolve continually to support new operating systems and recent releases. Also, they require high quality software artifacts to minimize chances of financial losses due to software bugs. For instance, a critical software running on a web server cannot stop serving clients due to a software crash, or an out of memory error. This way, practical studies with the C preprocessor are helpful to understand common problems, detect bugs, provide insights for better tool support, increase software quality, and support evolution of program families.

2. Problem

Developers use the C preprocessor in well-known and widely used program families. It is an effective tool that allows developers to encompass any code fragment with preprocessor directives, even a single token. However, they should be careful when using the C preprocessor to avoid bad smells in preprocessor directives [3]. For instance, *Gnuplot* developers annotate only part of an `if` statement with preprocessor directives as we can see in Listing 1 (Line 3). Notice that the correspondent closing bracket is at Line 10. It is an incomplete annotation, i.e., directives that encompass only parts of C syntactical units [4]. Incomplete annotations are bad smells in preprocessor directives because of their negative impact on code quality, e.g., developers may need more time to reason about the code, to detect where `if` statements end or to analyze whether opening and closing brackets match correctly [2, 5].

SPLASH '14, October 20–24, 2014, Portland, OR, USA.
Copyright is held by the owner/author(s).
ACM 978-1-4503-3208-8/14/10.
http://dx.doi.org/10.1145/10.1145/2660252.2660254

Listing 1. Code snippet of *Gnuplot* with bad smells.

```
1.  if (*Y_AXIS.label.text) {
2.  #ifdef PM3D
3.      if (rot_x <= 90){
4.  #endif
5.      double step = (other_end - yaxis_x) / 4;
6.      // Several lines of code..
7.  #ifdef PM3D
8.      if (map)
9.          *t = text_angle;
10.     }
11. #endif
12. }
```

Researchers propose refactorings to remove incomplete annotations [4, 9], but they clone code as we can see in Listing 2. It clones the list of statements at Lines 5 and 11. Thus, the proposed refactorings remove incomplete annotations by introducing another bad smell, i.e., code clone [3].

Listing 2. Existing refactoring to remove bad smells.
```
1.  if (*Y_AXIS.label.text) {
2.  #ifdef PM3D
3.      if (rot_x <= 90){
4.          double step = (other_end - yaxis_x) / 4;
5.          // Several lines of code..
6.          if (map)
7.              *t = text_angle;
8.      }
9.  #else
10.     double step = (other_end - yaxis_x) / 4;
11.     // Several lines of code..
12. #endif
13. }
```

Notice that the code snippet presented in Listing 1 contains no bugs. But it contains bad smells that eases the introduction of bugs related to variability [6, 7]. For instance, Listing 3 presents a newer version of the same code. However, developers introduce a bug when we do not define macro PM3D. By preprocessing the code of Listing 3 using this configuration, developers close a bracket at Line 8 without open its correspondent bracket at Line 3. Thus, we generate an invalid program that does not compile. But it compiles if we activate PM3D. Bugs related to variability are hard to detect because they happen only in specific configurations.

Listing 3. Code snippet of *Gnuplot* with a variability bug.
```
1.  if (*Y_AXIS.label.text) {
2.  #ifdef PM3D
3.      if (rot_x <= 90){
4.  #endif
5.      double step = (other_end - yaxis_x) / 4;
6.      // Several lines of code..
7.      if (map) { *t = text_angle; }
8.      }
9.  }
```

In particular, the majority of C development tools are not variability-aware. For instance, *GCC* and *Clang* preprocess the code and consider each family member individually. In academy, there are some variability-aware tools, e.g., *TypeChef* [5], which parses program families code and checks type errors. However, *TypeChef* uses a time-consuming strategy that needs to consider all external dependencies defined through #include directives. Despite of a few bug checkers in *TypeChef*, there are no variability-aware tools that focus on detecting different types of semantic bugs.

The strategy that considers each family member individually does not scale due to the high number of possible configurations. On the other hand, strategies that consider all external dependencies need a time-consuming set up to identify and install them. In addition, we have difficulties to install dependencies specific to a particular operating system. For instance, we cannot install *windows.h* in *Linux* since this library is not available for unix-based systems. Thus, without an appropriate tool support, developers introduce bad smells and bugs related to variability [1, 6, 7].

3. Approach

We propose an approach to safely evolve C program families, which supports developers to improve code quality, and detect bugs related to variability. In this context, we propose a catalogue of refactorings to remove bad smells in preprocessor directives, and a strategy to detect different bugs, such as syntax errors, null deferences, memory leaks, resource leaks, and uninitialized variables. Further, we develop a supporting tool named *Colligens*, which implements our strategy to detect bugs and applies our refactorings automatically.

Our refactorings are unidirectional transformation templates, which satisfy specific preconditions in order to minimize chances of introducing behavioural changes. In addition, they are simple and local transformations without global impact. But, we can compose them to perform different transformations. By removing bad smells, we improve code quality in the sense that the refactored code has preprocessor directives encompassing only complete C syntactical units. For instance, Refactoring 1 shows how we remove incomplete annotations in if wrappers. In this refactoring, we use an additional variable to keep the statement condition. To avoid compilation errors, we define a precondition that the code is not using identifier test in the scope. Notice that our refactoring does not clone code. Refactoring 2 implements runtime variability. Thus, after applying it, we have no directives. We use a local variable EXPR_RT to keep the value of macro EXPR. By applying Refactoring 1 or 2, we can remove the bad smells of *Gnuplot* presented before.

Refactoring 1. ⟨Remove incomplete if wrappers⟩

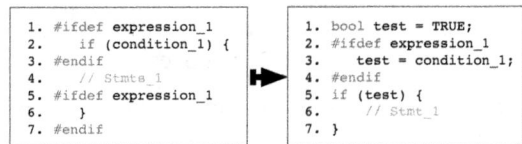

```
1.  #ifdef expression_1          1.  bool test = TRUE;
2.      if (condition_1) {       2.  #ifdef expression_1
3.  #endif                       3.      test = condition_1;
4.      // Stmts_1               4.  #endif
5.  #ifdef expression_1          5.  if (test) {
6.      }                        6.      // Stmt_1
7.  #endif                       7.  }
```

(→) variable test is not used in this scope.

Refactoring 2. ⟨Remove wrapper with runtime variability⟩

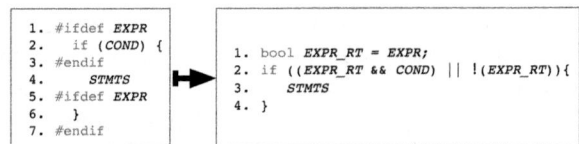

```
1.  #ifdef EXPR
2.      if (COND) {              1.  bool EXPR_RT = EXPR;
3.  #endif                       2.  if ((EXPR_RT && COND) || !(EXPR_RT)){
4.      STMTS                    3.      STMTS
5.  #ifdef EXPR                  4.  }
6.      }
7.  #endif
```

(→) variable EXPR_RT is not used in the code.

In some cases as depicted in Listing 3, bad smells may ease the introduction of bugs. Thus, we also define a strategy to detect bugs related to variability. To detect syntax errors, we use *TypeChef* to parse all family members, but we use stubs to substitute the external dependencies and avoid the time-consuming initial set up [5]. Figure 1 presents the steps of our strategy as discussed next. In *Step 1*, we exclude the external dependencies defined through #include directives and create the stubs. *Step 2* generates a script that calls *TypeChef* for each source file. In *Step 3*, we analyze the syntax errors to identify the ones related to variability. In the third step, we also get feedback from the actual program families developers to confirm the syntax errors.

To detect semantic bugs, our strategy uses a framework that allows the use of different sampling algorithms and static analysis tools. By sampling configurations and selecting only a few family members to analyze, we can use non-variability-aware tools that exist for several years, e.g., *CppCheck*[1] and *Splint*.[2] Figure 2 shows our strategy to detect semantic bugs. In *Step 1*, we use sampling to select a set of family members. Then, we use a static analysis tool to find bugs in *Step 2*. Notice that we can identify the same bug in different family members. Thus, *Step 3* removes duplicated bugs by analyzing their presence conditions.

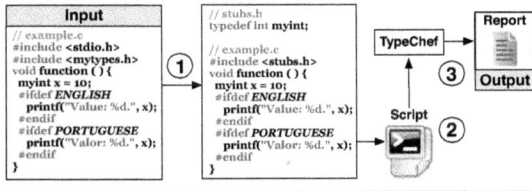

Figure 1. Detecting syntax errors in C program families.

4. Evaluation Methodology

Our goal is to evaluate our approach with respect to its efficiency to remove bad smells and detect bugs related to variability. Thus, we address the following research questions: **Q1.** Can our approach detect bugs related to variability? **Q2.** Which sampling algorithm finds the highest number of bugs? **Q3.** Can our approach detect and remove bad smells in preprocessor directives without clone source code? **Q4.** Does our catalogue of refactorings improve code understanding and maintainability? **Q5.** Why do developers still use preprocessor directives instead of runtime variability?

Planning. We plan to select families of different domains and sizes. To answer question **Q1**, we intend to perform an empirical study. To confirm that we detect real bugs, we will ask developers. In question **Q2**, we plan to compare different sampling algorithms to analyze the ones that detect the highest number of bugs. To answer question **Q3**, we intend to use our tool to detect and remove bad smells. Regarding questions **Q4** and **Q5**, we plan to send questionnaires and do interviews with real developers to find out whether they would use our refactorings. **Threats to validity.** We minimize threats related to construct validity by getting feedback from developers to confirm the bugs detected in our study. Our strategy excludes #include directives to eliminate external libraries in order to scale. Notice that we may face false negatives and positives. However, we minimize false positives using developers feedback. To minimize threats related to external validity, we select families of different sizes, ranging from 4.9 thousand to 1.5 million lines of code, and distinct domains, e.g., web servers and databases.

---

[1] http://cppcheck.sourceforge.net/

[2] http://www.splint.org/

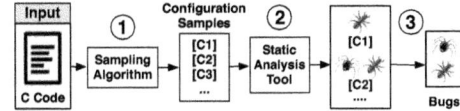

Figure 2. Detecting semantic bugs in C program families.

5. Research Status

Preliminary results. (**Q1**) By analyzing 40 families, we detect 121 bugs. We submit patches to fix bugs and developers accepted 78% of them. The majority of patches rejected were related to invalid configurations. (**Q2**) We implement different sampling algorithms to compare the number of bugs detected, e.g., t-wise. (**Q3**) Regarding our refactorings, we evaluate it by removing 477 bad smells in 12 families without cloning code, and increasing in 0.04% the lines of code and in 2.10% the number of directives. We are currently analyzing whether the order we apply our refactorings impacts the resulting code quality. **Future work.** So far, we have defined a strategy to detect bugs and refactorings to remove bad smells related to variability. We plan to analyze several sampling algorithms to detect bugs. Further, we intend to define a technique that avoids behavioural changes when applying our refactorings like in *SafeRefactor* [10]. Regarding **Q4**, we plan to evaluate the effectiveness of our refactorings by using a questionnaire. We will measure the impact of using incomplete annotations regarding code understandability and maintainability. In addition, we intend to do interviews to ask real program family developers whether they would use our catalogue of refactorings in practice. We will also use interviews to answer question **Q5**.

References

[1] I. Abal, C. Brabrand, and A. Wasowski. 40 variability bugs in the Linux kernel. Technical report, IT Univ. Copenhagen, Denmark, 2014.

[2] M. Ernst, G. Badros, and D. Notkin. An empirical analysis of C preprocessor use. *Trans. on Software Engineering*, 2002.

[3] M. Fowler. *Refactoring: Improving the Design of Existing Code*. Addison-Wesley, 1999.

[4] A. Garrido and R. Johnson. Analyzing multiple configurations of a C program. In *ICSM*, 2005.

[5] C. Kästner, P. Giarrusso, T. Rendel, S. Erdweg, K. Ostermann, and T. Berger. Variability-aware parsing in the presence of macros and conditional compilation. In *OOPSLA*, 2011.

[6] F. Medeiros, M. Ribeiro, and R. Gheyi. Investigating Preprocessor-Based Syntax Errors. In *GPCE*, 2013.

[7] F. Medeiros, M. Ribeiro, R. Gheyi, and B. Fonseca. A catalogue of refactorings to remove incomplete annotations. *Journal of Universal Computer Science*, January 2014.

[8] D. Parnas. On the design and development of program families. *IEEE Transactions on Software Engineering*, 1976.

[9] S. Schulze, J. Liebig, J. Siegmund, and S. Apel. Does the discipline of annotations matter? In *GPCE*, 2013.

[10] G. Soares, R. Gheyi, D. Serey, and T. Massoni. Making program refactoring safer. *IEEE Software*, 2010.

When Importless Becomes Meaningful:

A Call for Tag-based Namespaces in Programming Languages

Tomas Tauber

The University of Hong Kong
ttauber@cs.hku.hk

Abstract

Traditional programming language namespaces evolved from file-system structures. We describe different scenarios where this rigid code organization becomes a limiting factor. After that, we propose a more flexible code organization using tags. We then illustrate it on Python, including how we can convert existing code structures to the new tag-based one. Finally, we discuss our plans how to extend this work to statically typed languages in the future.

Categories and Subject Descriptors   D.3.3 [*Programming Languages*]: Language Constructs and Features – Modules, packages

Keywords   Modules; Packages; Tags; Namespaces; Python

1. Motivation

The way we do computer programming has not changed much over the last 40 years. Despite various improvements in development tools and new programming paradigms, we still store computer program source codes as static text files (except, for example, in JetBrains MPS[9]) in traditional hierarchical filesystems. This fact influences many design decisions in programming languages and their compilers.

One such decision is how we deal with naming collisions. Compilers scan all files on given local filesystem paths and complain if they find symbols with the same names. Programmers then need to rename these symbols, or make use of namespaces if their language supports this concept. In general, namespaces in programming languages have been more or less mimicking namespaces in hierarchical filesystems. Apart from a scoping role in language semantics and occasional meta-programming support, they do not differ much and suffer from similar problems:

- A program unit can only belong to one namespace. A class, a function or a constant can only belong to one module. A module can only belong to one package. In hierarchical namespaces, it may also belong to its parent packages, but it is still a restriction. A hierarchical code organization can be a suitable choice in a variety of cases and we do not argue against that. We rather argue that programmers or organizations should make this choice themselves.

- It assumes a traditional filesystem file as a base storage unit which may not be always meaningful. One could possibly create a file for each "program unit", but that may not be the best option. On the other hand, grouping different "program units" may not always make a semantic sense. Examples of that are "utility" or "commons" packages that tend to contain various pieces of different functionality. Reorganizing the code or temporarily grouping different parts of it in "virtual modules" may not be possible without using complex tools.

- Default querying, plain-text pattern matching, of text files is quite limiting. In filesystems, "desktop search engines" overcome this limitation. In programming languages, IDEs and various development tools allow better code searching or visualization. Even so, it is not an ideal situation and especially in dynamic languages, one can imagine how these tools would benefit from better querying support (e.g. more relevant code suggestions based on the surrounding code).

2. Problem

Beyond these inherent problems, we may encounter issues more relevant to software development:

- Programs contain semantic information that is being ignored, but may be useful for code organization and dependencies, querying, or visualization: information about versions, dependencies (e.g. a language version), authors, actual functionality, or data structures. They, however, are not standard parts of languages and may be inconsistent which is a reason why language runtimes ignore such information. Again, IDEs and other development tools may still make use of it.

- Portability of program units may be reduced. Even though individual units, such as functions, may be independent of each other, they may have inherent dependencies arising from their placement. For example, if one tries to copy a part of a code and paste it either in an interactive command line interface or in a different module, it will probably not work: 1) there might be naming collisions with existing identifiers in the current namespace, 2) there might be "unknown" identifiers (of unimported modules) even though an interpreter could find such unique identifiers on given search paths.

- Interactions among program units change over time and the structure may stop making sense. MacCormack, Rusnak and Baldwin [5] studied design evolution of a commercial software product over time. They found out that software architects' original choices did not match interactions and component structures in later versions. We cannot foresee such architectural changes in the future and refactoring may be fairly complex due to the rigid namespace structure and compatibility requirements.

SPLASH '14,   October 20-24 2014, Portland, OR, USA.
Copyright is held by the owner/author(s).
ACM 978-1-4503-3208-8/14/10.
http://dx.doi.org/10.1145/2660252.2660257

- There are issues that the use of traditional namespaces will not resolve. For example, if we try to import two different versions of the same library, it will be impossible and we will need to use qualified names and disambiguate them using the filesystem paths. A similar issue is with the same version of a library targeting different versions of the language. We can resolve these issues using build systems and other tools, such as `virtualenv` in Python. Nonetheless, such solutions are rather ad-hoc workarounds due to the imposed namespace design restrictions.

To illustrate some of these issues, we consider the following simple example in Python:

```
from weather import get_data
from numpy import sum
  (... some code ...)
def avg_temp():
  data = get_data()
  avg = sum(data) / len(data)
  return avg
  (... some code ...)
```

If we try to move this function definition to a different module, there might be problems with name clashes or unimported names (if we do not copy the related import statements). And, for example, we cannot select a specific version of `numpy` when multiple versions exist on the search path.

3. Approach

The mentioned problems exist, because language designs do not address them and leave it to external tools. Newly proposed tag-based filesystems, such as TagFS [2] or hFAD [7], solve the inherent issues in operating systems. Inspired by them, we explore this idea in the context of programming language namespaces.

3.1 Concept

We can imagine it in a language that lacks an import (require, include etc.) statement and has an implicit "autoload" for all names from the search path. For dynamic languages, this is trivial if a name referenced in a code is unique (e.g. `len()`). It may not be correct, but we do not get many guarantees anyway and it stresses the importance of testing. Statically typed languages require a more careful treatment and we will address them in the future work. Now, let us consider a scenario with non-unique names. We first need to perform "name mangling" of the colliding identifiers and keep track of these symbols. The question is then how to disambiguate.

As shown below, we annotate different parts of code with tags in comments. These tags not only describe functionality, but also potential dependencies and implicitly guide loading by ranking the overlap of tags. For instance, `get_data()` may be defined in `weather` and `stock_exchange` libraries and they provide different functionality. Tags `#weather` and `#temperature` appear in the former one, hence the function loads from there.

For `sum()`, we may have multiple options: Python's standard library, our own definition or other packages, such as `numpy`. All `sum()` definitions provide more or less the same functionality and may contain the same set of tags (e.g. `#summation`). In this case, we need to be more specific and provide more tags, either on the function definition level or before the call. For our definition, for example, we could add `#author:NAME`. If there are no more tags, we can then either modify the original definition and decorate it with more tags, or if that is not desirable, we can retag it locally:

```
# #weather #average #temperature
# #@#('.../site-packages/numpy/', #ndarray)
def avg_temp():
```

```
  data = get_data()
  # #summation #ndarray #version:1.8.1
  avg = sum(data) / len(data)
  return avg
```

One advantage this code organization brings is self-documentation. Naturally, different people may give different tags to the same code, but as with existing code organizations, this issue should be addressed in coding conventions of particular projects. Other advantages are that it helps to address the mentioned issues: we gain a greater flexibility in code organization; we can index program units by their tags and by names they import; we can reorganize the code by generating temporary "workspace" virtual modules containing code that matches a query; program units carry all their dependencies locally; we may have different versions of the same library on the search path and disambiguate based on tags, such as `#version:1.0` or `#pythonversion:2.7`.

Such tag-based "importless" schemes can be retrofitted as preprocessors to most language runtimes of current dynamic languages. We demonstrate it on CPython 2.7.6.

3.2 Tagging

There are three levels at which we can tag our code:

1. **Top**: This level includes classes, functions or variables defined in a global scope. For classes and functions, everything in their scope has at least the surrounding set of tags. These annotations are not only guiding imports in that scope, but are also exposing how particular units can be referenced and used.

2. **Block**: Python does not have code blocks on their own, so we refer to control-flow constructs: `while`, `if-elif-else`, `for`, `try-except-finally`, and `with-as`. We can annotate a control flow block and all its statements may gain tags in addition to the ones defined at the surrounding top-level.

3. **Statement**: Finally, we can annotate individual statements on their preceding lines.

From the code organization perspective, we use the block- and statement-level tagging for isolated disambiguation that does not interfere with the rest of the code. We could, however, still use it to guide code searching – i.e. we can extract and index tags from all levels for a particular unit, but we may want to assign them with different weights.

3.3 Converting Existing Hierarchies

We adopt the following procedure to convert existing code structures:

- Given a source file, annotate each top-level unit with tags generated from its module name and all its parent packages. All imported modules and their parent packages generate tags that annotate a corresponding level, i.e. all top-level units (if in the beginning of the module) or the enclosing scope of a particular block (if it is a local import statement).

- For all references to names from the standard library, annotate their preceding lines with a tag `#__builtin__`.

- For all import statements, remove module prefixes of each reference and annotate its preceding line with the module name tag.

- For all import-as statements, generate retagging statements with paths to these modules and tags from aliases. Remove each alias prefix and annotate its preceding line with the corresponding tag.

- Tag any-module level executable code blocks with `#__main__`.

- Remove all import statements.

This approach is basic and possible future work can improve upon it by extracting keywords and annotations from docstrings and annotating corresponding parts of code with them.

3.4 Storing and Editing

For the ease of querying, we store top-level units and their tags in a relational database. We can achieve it using two tables (or three if a more normalized solution is desirable): the first table stores names, "description" (class, function, variable), mangled names, paths, and actual code; the second one references the first table and stores corresponding tags for each unit. We can then specify temporary file names and what code they should contain based on tags. A tool, running in the background, can continuously watch changes in these files (e.g. via *inotify*) and sync changes with the database by diffs: update or delete code, add or remove tags, update names and regenerate the mangled names, or add new entries.

3.5 Loading

The interpreter runs a code block specified by a name and tags. For the code execution, we essentially follow the reverse conversion process in pre-processing (using Python's `tokenize`) and regenerate original code organization: we infer explicit imports from tags and insert them to code along with possible module or qualified name prefixes. There may be program code that was added to temporary files and does not have a physical filesystem location. We dump all such units into a single temporary module under their mangled names. We then add import statements for this temporary module to files that are referencing these units and replace the names with the mangled names in them.

In order to support dynamic code (`exec`, `eval` or command-line interface), we need to modify Python's internals on initialization and add an exception hook (`sys.excepthook`) to handle *NameErrors*. When we catch a *NameError*, we query the database for a given name and try to resolve it; if we cannot resolve it, we raise an error and print all matching names along with their tags.

4. Evaluation Methodology

The primary hypothesis is that it is possible to use the more flexible tag-based namespaces instead of the traditional hierarchical namespaces in a dynamic language without sacrificing "code quality". The secondary hypothesis is that while using this code organization, one can still achieve a comparable performance.

We are going to test these hypotheses on a converted bundle of existing popular packages. In particular, we plan to convert packages from the Anaconda 1.9.2 collection. For the primary hypothesis, we compare cohesions of modules before the conversion and of corresponding virtual modules. We use the LCOM4 metric [3] on the module level (rather than the class level) to assess the cohesion.

For the secondary hypothesis, we utilize Python's `timeit` module to measure execution time. As a baseline, we first measure runtime performance of multiple runs of unit tests for each unconverted package. In order to gain consistent steady-state results, we execute 3 warm-up runs before running 10 measured runs, and force garbage collection before each run. We measure in this setting for each package's unit test collection in separate VM invocations. We will follow the same procedure with the tag-namespace aware interpreter executing on the converted packages.

5. Related Work

The closest to this work is keyword programming [4]. In keyword programming, users provide unordered keywords which are then translated into queries against APIs and search results generate detailed expressions in the given code context. In attribute-oriented programming [6], programmers mark parts of programs to indicate application- or domain-specific semantics and preprocessors generate more detailed programs for these annotated parts. Namespaces, however, remain the same as in the original language (Java).

Other generative and metaprogramming paradigms, such as intentional programming [1], allow programmers to create code in a higher level of abstraction. They also address the issues related to productivity by making program code more accessible for tools. These approaches often imply a completely new programming model which may not be easily retrofitted to existing languages.

UpgradeJ [8] was an extension to the Java programming language that focused on the problem of dynamic software updating (hotswapping). It provides an explicit upgrade mechanism and allows multiple versions of the same classes to co-exist in the same namespace by forcing class names to be annotated with a version number.

6. Future Work

After finishing the prototype for dynamic languages, we would like to extend this work to statically typed languages. We need to examine the semantics of tag-based namespaces in this scenario. And we may need to extend the current scheme: attaching weights to tags, different ways of combining them or defining relationships among them, such as different restrictions on which tags can co-exist in the same annotation sets. Under this defined semantics, we will explore the possibility of type inference. In addition to it, we will look into how tag-based namespaces can be combined with existing programming paradigms – for instance, how tags should be exposed and propagated with respect to notions of ownership and inheritance in OOP.

References

[1] W. Aitken, B. Dickens, P. Kwiatkowski, O. D. Moor, D. Richter, and C. Simonyi. Transformation in intentional programming. *Proceedings. Fifth International Conference on Software Reuse (Cat. No.98TB100203)*, 1998. ISSN 1085-9098. .

[2] S. Bloehdorn, O. Görlitz, S. Schenk, M. Völkel, and F. I. Karlsruhe. Tagfs - tag semantics for hierarchical file systems. In *I-KNOW 06: Proceedings of the 6th International Conference on Knowledge Management*, pages 6–8, 2006. .

[3] M. Hitz and B. Montazeri. Measuring Coupling and Cohesion In Object-Oriented Systems. *Angewandte Informatik*, 50:1–10, 1995. URL http://www.isys.uni-klu.ac.at/PDF/1995-0043-MHBM.pdf.

[4] G. Little and R. C. Miller. Keyword programming in Java. *Automated Software Engineering*, 16(1):37–71, Oct. 2008. ISSN 0928-8910. . URL http://link.springer.com/10.1007/s10515-008-0041-9.

[5] A. MacCormack, J. Rusnak, and C. Baldwin. *The Impact of Component Modularity on Design Evolution: Evidence from the Software Industry*. 2007. . URL http://www.ssrn.com/abstract=1071720.

[6] D. Schwarz. Peeking Inside the Box: Attribute-Oriented Programming with Java 1.5, 2004. URL http://www.onjava.com/pub/a/onjava/2004/06/30/insidebox1.html.

[7] M. Seltzer and N. Murphy. Hierarchical File Systems are Dead. *Applied Sciences*, page 1, 2009. URL http://portal.acm.org/citation.cfm?id=1855569.

[8] E. Tempero, G. Bierman, J. Noble, and M. Parkinson. From Java to UpgradeJ. In *Proceedings of the 1st International Workshop on Hot Topics in Software Upgrades - HotSWUp '08*, page 1, New York, New York, USA, Oct. 2008. ACM Press. ISBN 9781605583044. . URL http://dl.acm.org/citation.cfm?id=1490283.1490285.

[9] M. Völter and V. Pech. Language modularity with the MPS language workbench. In *IEEE 34th International Conference on Software Engineering (ICSE)*, pages 1449–1450. IEEE, 2012. ISBN 978-1-4673-1067-3. .

SPLASH 2014 Demo Chairs' Welcome

OCTOBER 19–24

SPLASH

PORTLAND 2014

It is our great pleasure to welcome you to Portland and the 2014 SPLASH Demonstration track! We all know that it's better to see something once than to hear about it a hundred times. Live demonstrations show the impact of software innovation in a dynamic and highly interactive setting. This track is an excellent opportunity for companies and universities to share their latest work with an experienced and technically savvy audience: you.

We have received many interesting and diverse demonstration submissions from both industry and academia, and have compiled an exciting demonstration program consisting of tools, applications, and languages in various stages of development – from prototypes and proofs of concept to mature tools and systems. Each of them contains interesting and relevant technology and should appeal to the SPLASH community.

These demonstrations are not product sales pitches, but rather an opportunity for the authors to highlight, explain, and present interesting technical aspects of running applications. The sessions are intended to be two-way interactions with the audience, which has the opportunity to share ideas, interact with the authors in a small-scale venue, and learn techniques used in developing innovative and high quality software.

We would like to thank this year's demonstration presenters for their hard work in bringing live demonstrations to SPLASH 2014. We are also grateful to this year's demonstrations subcommittee for their efforts to shape the 2014 demonstrations program. Finally we would like to thank you for attending this session and for all the feedback given to the authors.

Floréal Morandat
Demonstration Chair
LaBRI / Bordeaux University

Pocket Code: A Scratch-like Integrated Development Environment for your Phone

Wolfgang Slany
Institute of Software Technology
Graz University of Technology
Austria, Europe
+43-316-873-5721
wolfgang.slany@tugraz.at

ABSTRACT

In our free open source project Catrobat, we are developing Pocket Code, an integrated development environment (IDE) for a visual, Lego-block style programming language that is inspired by MIT's Scratch. In contrast to Scratch and AppInventor, Pocket Code is designed to completely run on smartphones – no PC whatsoever is needed to develop or execute the programs. Our motivation is to allow teenagers to intuitively create and easily share their own mobile apps. The large project includes more than 20 subprojects that complement Pocket Code in various ways, e.g., an image editor app that supports transparency and zooming up to pixel level. According to Ohloh, as of June 2014 more than 371 person years have been invested by 270 volunteer contributors from more than 20 countries into Catrobat. All development is done in an agile, extremely iterative and test-driven way, with a strong focus on maintainability, usability, and design. Subteams in parallel develop native versions of Catrobat interpreters that are integrated into corresponding Pocket Code IDEs for the Android, iOS, and Windows Phone platforms as well as for HTML5 capable mobile browsers, or smartphones supporting HTML5 directly. These native versions are implemented by us respectively in Java, ObjectiveC, C# & C++, and HTML5/JavaScript. I will demonstrate Pocket Code and also will show how we use automatically checkable specification to ensure that programs behave identically on all platforms even though no cross-compilation tools or common implementation languages are used.

Categories and Subject Descriptors

D.1.7 [**Programming Techniques**]: Visual Programming.

Keywords

Visual programming, kids, teenagers, smartphones, mobile app, computer science education, STEM.

SPLASH '14 Companion, Oct 20-24 2014, Portland, OR, USA
ACM 978-1-4503-3208-8/14/10.
http://dx.doi.org/10.1145/2660252.2664662

Short Biography

Wolfgang Slany is the head and founder of the Catrobat project that develops Pocket Code since 2010. He is a full professor of computer science and head of the Institute for Software Technology at Graz University of Technology. His research topics include software quality, agile development and project management, computer science education, visual programming, interaction design, and mobile development systems.

```
Scenario: A waiting BroadcastAndWait brick is
  unblocked via another BroadcastAndWait brick.

  Object 'test object' has the following scripts:

    when program started
      broadcast 'Print b after 0.2 seconds' and wait
      print 'a'

    when program started
      wait 0.1 seconds
      broadcast 'Print b after 0.2 seconds' and wait
      print 'c'

    when I receive 'Print b after 0.2 seconds'
      wait 0.2 seconds
      print 'b'

  When I start the program
  And I wait until the program has stopped
  Then I should see the printed output 'abc'
```

Listing 1. An assertion describing how BroadcastAndWait bricks should behave in a particular situation.

Listing 1 shows one out of many test cases for the building blocks of the Catrobat language written in a Gherkin-like syntax. The Gherkin syntax has been slightly adapted for Catrobat in order to make the specification of programs more readable. These test cases are written manually and are automatically translated into unit- and functional tests for each platform, where they are also automatically integrated into the respective test-suites. The tests fulfill many functions: They are a developer-friendly documentation of the semantics of the Catrobat language, provide regression-test type protection against misunderstandings arising during refactorings before adding new features (frequent as the project is highly iterative, with many ever-changing contributors), provides a declarative executable specification that can be used when implementing another, new interpreter or compiler for the Catrobat language, and directly is supportive of our test-driven-development style.

Note that our test cases among others also include hardware based functional tests for built-in sensors (e.g., inclination and NFC sensors), effectors (e.g., flash and vibration), sound and camera, wireless connections to Bluetooth based Arduino boards, Lego Mindstorms robots, Parrot AR.Drones, and a few other toy robots, e.g., WowWee's RoboMe.

Catrobat allows creating, sharing, and remixing one's own games and interactive animations (see Figure 2). New features, e.g., a 2D physics engine, are continuously being added.

Acknowledgements: See http://catrob.at/credits and http://developer.catrobat.org/special_thanks

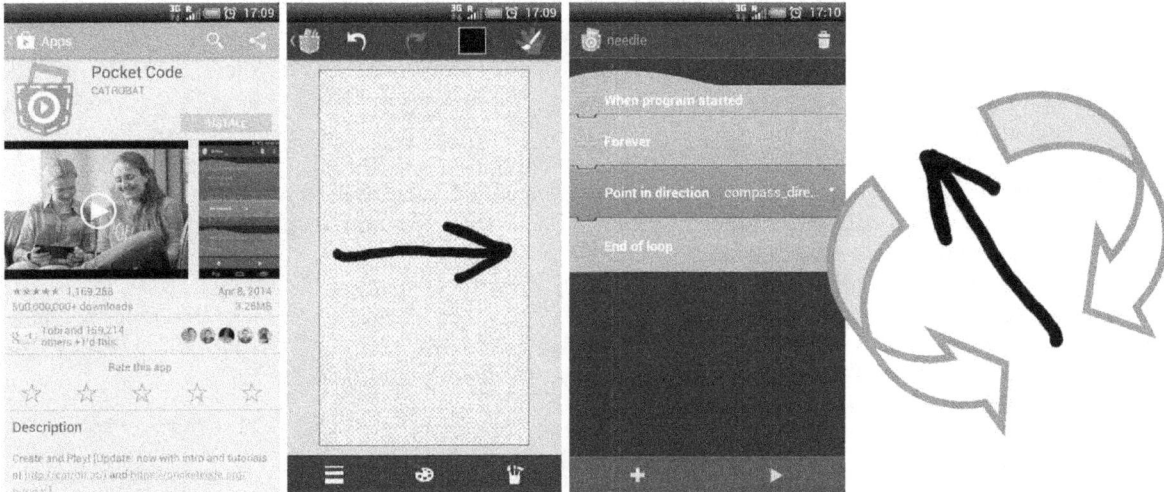

Figure 1. Pocket Code allows going from installing it to creating, e.g., a fully functional compass app in less than one minute.

Figure 2. Upload, share, and remix programs made with Pocket Code.

OMEN: A Tool for Synthesizing Tests for Deadlock Detection [*]

Malavika Samak [†]

Indian Institute of Science, Bangalore
malavika@csa.iisc.ernet.in

Murali Krishna Ramanathan [‡]

Indian Institute of Science, Bangalore
muralikrishna@csa.iisc.ernet.in

Abstract

Designing and implementing *thread-safe* multithreaded libraries can be a daunting task as developers of these libraries need to ensure that their implementations are free from concurrency bugs, including deadlocks. Developing multithreaded tests for this purpose is significantly challenging. In this demo, we will demonstrate our tool (OMEN) for synthesizing deadlock-inducing multithreaded tests for Java libraries. The input to OMEN is the library implementation under consideration and the output is a set of deadlock revealing multithreaded tests.

1. Introduction

Thread-safe [3] libraries are beneficial as the developers of the client programs need not consider the intricacies of the issues pertaining to multithreading and yet accrue the benefits of multithreading. However, designing such libraries can be challenging.

```
class A {                     class Test {
    synchronized foo (A a) {      void testFoo(A a1, A a2) {
        synchronized (a) {}           a1.foo(a2)
    }                             }
}                             }
```

Figure 1. Illustrative example.

Consider the simple example shown in Figure 1. It presents the implementation of method foo in class A. When a client, testFoo, invokes foo as shown in the figure, a lock on a_1 is acquired followed by a lock on a_2. The

[*] An extended version is published at OOPSLA 2014 [4].

[†] 3rd year PhD student and the lead developer of OMEN.

[‡] Assistant Professor. Formerly, a member of the core analysis team at Coverity, San Francisco, USA.

implementation of A is *not* thread-safe because a deadlock can occur under certain scenarios when foo is called without holding appropriate lock(s). For example, if two threads invoke testFoo(a_1,a_2) and testFoo(a_2,a_1) concurrently, then a deadlock may manifest in some execution. This is because the first thread may attempt to acquire a lock on a_2 while holding a lock on a_1 and the second thread may attempt to acquire a lock on a_1 while holding a lock on a_2.

If testFoo is executed by a single thread, a dynamic deadlock detector[1, 5] will not detect any deadlock in the corresponding execution. If we synthesize method sequences that can be executed concurrently in a *random* manner and have the deadlock detector analyze the corresponding execution, it will not necessarily be helpful either. For example, invoking a_1.foo(a_2) from different threads cannot help because the threads do not acquire the locks in opposite order. For the deadlock to manifest, it is essential that different threads invoke foo as explained in the previous paragraph. Unfortunately, even for such a simple example, the sophisticated machinery of deadlock detectors fail to detect any problems, unless a suitable test case exists.

In general, deadlocks can occur if a combination of certain methods are invoked by different threads. A brute force analysis of concurrent execution of different possible combination of methods [3] is impractical. Even assuming that the relevant combination of methods to be executed concurrently is provided by an oracle, the *invocation context* becomes vital to detect any issues.

2. Architecture

We address the problem of synthesizing multithreaded test cases to enable deadlock detection in multithreaded libraries [4]. Our key insight is that a subset of properties (e.g., nested lock acquisitions) that are exhibited when a deadlock manifests in a multithreaded execution can also be observed in a single threaded execution. Subsequently, we use the observed properties to enable the synthesis of a deadlock revealing multithreaded test case. Based on this insight, we propose a novel, directed and scalable approach for synthesizing multithreaded test cases. We have implemented a tool, named OMEN, on top of the soot [6] bytecode analysis framework that incorporates our approach.

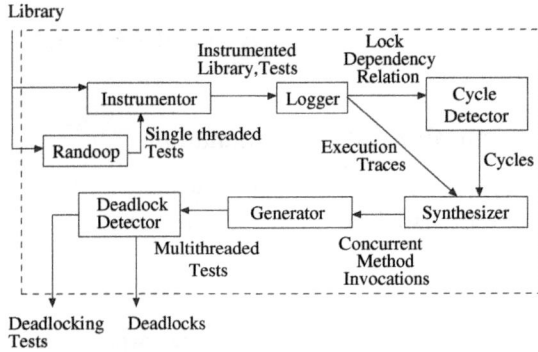

Figure 2. Architecture of OMEN.

The overall architecture of our tool, OMEN [4], for synthesizing multithreaded test cases to enable deadlock detection is given in Figure 2. There are four major components in our design: Logger, Cycle Detector, Synthesizer and Generator. The input to OMEN is the library under consideration. If the seed testsuite (manually developed single threaded tests) is not given as input, we generate the seed testsuite using Randoop [2]. The Instrumentor instruments the library and the tests. The Logger executes the instrumented tests and stores the execution traces. It also constructs a *lock dependency relation* across the execution of all test cases in the testsuite and inputs it to the Cycle Detector. The Cycle Detector detects the presence of cyclic chains in the dependency relation. A cycle suggests the possibility of a deadlock when the corresponding test cases are executed concurrently. However, executing the identified test cases concurrently is not enough as the threads need to acquire locks on *shared* objects in a conflicting order. The Synthesizer processes the detected cycles and the execution traces to synthesize possible sets of concurrent method invocations. These invocations when made by different threads may manifest a deadlock. For each set of invocations, the Generator constructs a multithreaded test case by spawning threads and performing each invocation in the set from a different thread. These tests are executed and analyzed by iGoodLock [1] which reports the detected deadlocks along with the corresponding multithreaded tests.

3. Evaluation

We analyze multithreaded Java libraries to evaluate OMEN. All the experiments are conducted on an Ubuntu-12.04 desktop running on a 3.5 Ghz Intel Core i7 processor with 16GB RAM. We are able to detect a number of unknown (and known) deadlocks by applying OMEN on many multithreaded Java libraries. We use the automatically generated tests from Randoop [2] as the seed testsuite and are able to generate 26 multithreaded tests from a total of 3500 sequential tests. Table 1 presents the benchmarks along with information on the number of tests synthesized for each

Class name	Tests	DL	TP
DynamicBin1D	6	36	21
CharArrayWriter	1	1	1
ClosableByteArrayOutputStream	1	1	1
ClosableCharArrayWriter	1	1	1
HashTable	15	20	19
Stack	1	1	1
ByteArrayOutputStream	1	1	1
Total	26	61	45

Table 1. Experimental results. DL: Deadlocks, TP: True Positives.

benchmark. Analyzing the execution traces of the synthesized tests detects 61 deadlocks across all libraries, including 45 true positives. In comparison, ConTeGe [3] randomly invokes methods concurrently and generates approximately 27K multithreaded tests and is unable to detect *any* deadlock. The difference in the numbers shows the contrast between randomized and directed approaches. More interestingly, we also detected the possibility of deadlocks in classes in colt, a library for high performance scientific computing, that are *documented* as thread safe. The overall analysis time of OMEN is negligible. For example, the analysis time for a trace with one million elements (DynamicBin1D) is seven minutes approximately.

4. Related Work

In ConTeGe [3], the authors describe a design for randomly generating method invocations that can be executed concurrently. Subsequently, if a concurrent execution results in an exception and none of the corresponding linearized executions fail, then a thread safety violation is reported. As we discuss in Section 3, their approach invokes methods randomly and the search space can be significant. Many dynamic analysis approaches [1, 5, 7] are designed for detecting deadlocks. All these approaches are fundamentally dependent on the quality of the analyzed executions to efficiently detect deadlocks. This is dependent on the quality of the tests. Our approach for automatically synthesizing multithreaded test cases *complements* these techniques.

References

[1] P. Joshi, C.-S. Park, K. Sen, and M. Naik. A randomized dynamic program analysis technique for detecting real deadlocks. PLDI '09.

[2] C. Pacheco and M. D. Ernst. Randoop: Feedback-directed random testing for java. OOPSLA '07.

[3] M. Pradel and T. R. Gross. Fully automatic and precise detection of thread safety violations. PLDI '12.

[4] M. Samak and M. K. Ramanathan. Multithreaded test synthesis for deadlock detection. OOPSLA '14.

[5] M. Samak and M. K. Ramanathan. Trace driven dynamic deadlock detection and reproduction. PPoPP '14.

[6] R. Vallee-Rai, E. Gagnon, L. Hendren, P. Lam, P. Pominville, and V. Sundaresan. Optimizing java bytecode using the soot framework: Is it feasible? CC '00.

[7] C. Yan, W. Shangru, and W. K. Chan. Conlock: A constraint-based approach to dynamic checking on deadlocks in multithreaded programs. ICSE '14.

Agile Programming with Executable Models
An Open-Source, Standards-Based Eclipse Environment

Ed Seidewitz

Model Driven Solutions
14000 Gulliver's Trail
Bowie MD 20720 USA
+1.301.4555.3681
ed-s@modeldriven.com

Arnaud Cuccuru

CEA Saclay - NanoInnov
PC 174
91191 Gif sur Yvette Cedex
France
arnaud.cuccuru@cea.fr

Abstract

Why can it be so hard to extract the "truth" from the code, especially on important big-picture, architectural issues in large systems? Models designed for human understanding can display these things much more clearly, but how do you keep the models in sync with the code? Well, suppose the model *was* the code – then you could have the best of both worlds! This is, indeed, possible, as is demonstrated using a combination of standard UML graphical class modeling and standard Alf action language programming, all based on a common, standard executable semantic foundation, new capabilities implemented in the Eclipse Papyrus UML tool. The result is a step toward a next generation agile programming environment.

Categories and Subject Descriptors   D.2.10 [**Software Engineering**]: Design – *methodologies*, D.3.2 [**Programming Languages**]: Language Classifications – *design languages, object-oriented languages*

General Terms   Design, Standardization, Languages

Keywords   Executable modeling, UML, action languages

1. The Problem

In agile development we value "working software over comprehensive documentation" [8]. Working software does what it does, and it either provides demonstrable value or it does not. Documentation in the absence of working software can often be open to interpretation and often not up to date. Code itself provides the "single source of truth" on working software. A disciplined agile approach puts a lot of effort into making sure that code is well structured and understandable. Summary documentation can be generated directly from the code if necessary.

So, even agile software developers often use some sort of models in order to discuss such issues. Domain or architectural models may be sketched early in a project, or they may be reverse-engineered from the code in order to deal with specific problems later. They are then discarded once they have served their purpose of aiding the creation of solutions that can be captured in code.

But this can result in multiple cycles of externalizing into models the architectural and domain abstractions implicit in code, then updating and re-capturing them in code, only to have to repeat the cycle as the need arises again and again. This process can be needlessly expensive and may still not provide a complete picture of the original intensions of the problem and solution architectures captured in the code.

There must be a better way. Suppose we could actually execute models without having to rewrite them in a traditional programming language. Then the model could *be* the code *and* be documentation of it.

2. The Solution

Indeed, there has actually been a long-standing minority in the software development community who created models precise enough that they could be executed in their own right. Such approaches date back to at least the 80s and 90s, including the Shlear-Mellor method [16][17], Real-Time Object-Oriented Modeling (ROOM) [15] and Harel Statecharts [7]. (In fact, Stephen Mellor. was a signatory to the Agile Manifesto.) However, commercial executable modeling tools supporting such approaches have long ago converted over to standard Unified Modeling Language (UML) notations [14].

While UML is a widely recognized and used general purpose modeling language, the majority of the programming

OOPSLA'14, October 20–24, 2014, Portland, Oregon, USA.
ACM 978-1-4503-2585-1/14/10.
http://dx.doi.org/10.1145/2660252.2664664

community generally still considers UML modeling to be "just drawing pictures". The high-level nature of most UML modeling, and the lack of precision in the specification of UML itself, means that the "real" programs still needed to be coded in some regular programming language. Perhaps some of this code was generated from the UML models, but it was the target code that was usually visible and considered executable by the developer.

Recently, however, there has been an increase in interest in executable modeling within the OMG membership. This has led to two new specifications adopted by the OMG, the *Semantics of a Foundational Subset for Executable UML Models* (fUML) [12] and the *Action Language for Foundational UML* (Alf) [13]. The demonstration will show how these standards are being realized in the Papyrus UML tool, providing an open-source environment for executable modeling – essentially programming in UML.

3. The Demonstration

Papyrus is a full-featured, open-source UML tool under the Eclipse Modeling Project [3]. The demonstration presents the executable modeling capabilities being developed for Papyrus, including:

- Creating a complete program as a graphical UML class model, with detailed behavioral code written textually using Alf.

- Synchronizing the graphical representation of a UML class with its textual representation in Alf.

- Concurrent execution of UML activities.

- Animating the execution of an activity.

- Debugging an executing activity.

The implementation of this environment is built on a number of existing Eclipse implementations of other foundational OMG standards:

- Papyrus 1.0.0 uses the Eclipse UML2 implementation [5] of UML 2.5 [14] and provides a fUML execution plugin (in incubation) based on it.

- An Ecore [1] metamodel for Alf was generated from the Alf metamodel, which is normatively defined using OMG's Meta Object Facility (MOF) [10].

- Static-semantic constraints in Alf are specified using OMG's Object Constraint Language (OCL) [11] and evaluated in real-time as text is entered [2].

- The abstract syntax tree for Alf text is mapped to the UML abstract syntax using OMG's MOF Query/View/Transformation (QVT) [9] operational language [4].

- The editing and parsing of Alf text is implemented using the Xtext domain specific language technology [6], which provides typical Eclipse editor capabilities.

The execution of models in Papyrus is currently intended more as a simulation of a system under development, rather than as the end delivery platform. However, this still provides the ability to fully implement and test the system at the model level. Papyrus and Eclipse capabilities for code generation can then be used to generate target-platform executable code.

But the goal remains to keep the UML model as the primary, executable artifact for any continued development and testing. No need to regenerate UML in order to see the big picture – that is just part of the code! And Alf provides a more traditional textual code representation when that is more convenient, especially for detailed behavioral code.

Any target code generation then just becomes a final compilation step. As the quality of target compilation from fUML improves, the generated code will be of no more concern to the programmer than is the object code from today's mainstream programming languages. And so we will finally move up another generation in the level of abstraction at which we are able to program.

Acknowledgments

Work on the integration of Alf into Papyrus was supported by the French Commissariat à l'Energie Atomique et aux Energies Alternatives (CEA), which also provides the lead for the development of Papyrus tooling in general.

References

[1] https://www.eclipse.org/modeling/emf/?project=emf#emf

[2] https://projects.eclipse.org/projects/modeling.mdt.ocl

[3] https://www.eclipse.org/papyrus/

[4] https://projects.eclipse.org/projects/modeling.mmt.qvt-oml

[5] https://projects.eclipse.org/projects/modeling.mdt.uml2

[6] https://www.eclipse.org/Xtext/

[7] Harel, D. and Politi, M., 1998. *Modeling Reactive Systems with Statecharts: The Statement Approach*. McGraw-Hill.

[8] http://agilemanifesto.org.

[9] http://www.omg.org/spec/QVT/1.1

[10] http://www.omg.org/spec/MOF/2.4.1

[11] http://www.omg.org/spec/OCL/2.3.1

[12] http://www.omg.org/spec/FUML/1.1

[13] http://www.omg.org/spec/ALF/1.0.1

[14] http://www.omg.org/spec/UML/2.5/Beta2

[15] Selic, B., Gullekson, G. and Ward. P., 1994. *Real-Time Object-Oriented Modeling*. Wiley.

[16] Shlaer, S. and Mellor, S. J., 1988.*Object-Oriented Systems Analysis: Modeling the World in Data*. Prentice Hall.

[17] Shlaer, S. and Mellor, S. J., 1991. *Object Lifecycles: Modeling the World in States*. Prentice Hall.

East Meets West: The Influences of Geography on Software Production

Steven Fraser

Independent Consultant
Research Relations & Tech Transfer
sdfraser@acm.org

Dennis Mancl

Member of Technical Staff
Alcatel-Lucent
dennis.mancl@alcatel-lucent.com

Aki Namioka

Search Engineering Team Manager
Marchex
anamioka@marchex.com

Roberto Salama

Director
Millennium Partners
roberto.salama@gmail.com

Allen Wirfs-Brock

Mozilla Corporation
allenwb@mozilla.com

Abstract

How do software development practices differ from coast-to-coast? What should practitioners learn about the influences of geography – and why is it important?

Each community of software professionals has its own technical biases: preferred programming languages, software tools, design paradigms, software testing approaches, and techniques for collaboration within a working group. Conferences like SPLASH provide an opportunity to compare notes, to learn from the successes (and failures) of others, to learn about new technologies, and to learn about how other groups communicate and collaborate.

This panel will focus on the diversity of software development practices in North America and the broader influences of geography.

Categories and Subject Descriptors K.6.1 [**Management of Computing and Information Systems**]: Project and People Management; K.7.2 [**The Computing Profession**]: Organizations.

General Terms Management.

Keywords Geography; organizational learning

SPLASH '14 Companion, Oct 20-24 2014, Portland, OR, USA
ACM 978-1-4503-3208-8/14/10.
http://dx.doi.org/10.1145/2660252.2661293

1. Steven Fraser

How do software development practices differ from coast-to-coast? Practitioners need to think about the influences of geography and culture on how they work with others. This panel will focus on the diversity of software development practices in North America and the broader influences of geography.

This panel brings together industry experts from east and west, to discuss topics including preferences for:

- Development tools and environments
- Embracing change – adopting new tools, automated techniques, etc.
- Agile and iterative development approaches
- Reuse assets, COTS, and open source components
- Software methods and quality trade-offs
- Teamwork and preferences for in-office, home-office, and remote-offices
- Innovation – through engineering, in-house research labs, external research, acquisitions
- Techniques for consolidating mergers and acquisitions
- Maximizing organizational learning – through internal conferences, instructor or peer led training, facilitated workshops, and eLearning (video based training, blogs, wikis, etc.)

STEVEN FRASER is an independent consultant on innovation and technology transfer. From 2007 to 2013, Steven was the Director of the Cisco Research Center. His achievements included: increasing the visibility and leverage of Cisco-university research collaborations, increasing the number of PhD/Post-Doc recruits, and accelerating technology transfer through the establishment of the Cisco Research Commons and the CTech Forum – a proprietary conference for Cisco Staff. Prior to joining Cisco, Steven was a Senior Staff member of Qualcomm's Learning Center in San Diego, leading software learning programs and creating the corporation's internal technical conference (the QTech Forum). Late in the last century, Steven held a variety of technology strategy roles at BNR/ Nortel including: Senior Manager (Disruptive Technology and Global External Research) and Advisor (Design Process Engineering). In 1994 he spent a year as a Visiting Scientist at the Software Engineering Institute (SEI) collaborating with the "Application of Software Models" project on the development of team-based domain analysis software reuse) techniques. Steven is a Senior Member of the ACM and the IEEE.

2. Dennis Mancl

The software industry requires its workers to be lifelong learners. Our patterns of work and our patterns of learning about technology are formed as much by our working environment as they are by courses and projects in our college and university training. It is in the work world where we begin to learn how to build commercial software products. We learn through many channels: collaboration with more experienced colleagues, picking up ideas from new staff members who transfer from another company, or doing some self-directed study to experiment with new languages, tools, and methods. I think that there are some significant differences in the patterns of lifelong learning across industries, technologies, and regions. There are some challenges when doing cross-industry or cross-location projects. We learn that different parts of the project team are making different product design tradeoffs or are advocating different development techniques. We must understand some of our own biases to do successful collaborative development.

DENNIS MANCL is a Member of Technical Staff at Alcatel-Lucent in Murray Hill, New Jersey, where he works on software tools and processes to support quality and productivity in the telecom industry. He has been working with technologies from C++ to UML to use cases to agile development in his years as an internal software process consultant for AT&T, Lucent, and Alcatel-Lucent.

3. Aki Namioka

There are a number of cross-cultural issues that can influence how well teams can work together and what tools they use. Ultimately, teams are made up of people, and people are influenced by several factors including their culture, their employers, their employment history, and their co-workers.

In my experience, working for both large multi-national companies and small local companies, there are challenges all over the place. Some examples that I will highlight are:

large vs. small companies, teams that are local vs. remote, agile vs. non-agile organizations, "western" vs. "eastern" cultures, and industry specific cultures.

AKI NAMIOKA has been working in high-tech since 1989. Her experience includes Boeing, IBM Global Services, and Cisco Systems. She is currently an Engineering Manager for the Seattle-based company Marchex, and has been an Agile Practitioner since 2002.

4. Roberto Salama

ROBERTO SALAMA has an MS in Electrical and Computer Engineering from North Carolina State University. He worked in the area of circuit simulation for a number of years before heading on to financial engineering. Over the last twenty years, Roberto has worked at Goldman Sachs and Morgan Stanley building systems ranging from Fixed Income trading systems to financial analysis interactive platforms to time series systems. His area of interest is the application of emerging technologies, especially in the areas of languages and distributed processing, to financial engineering.

5. Allen Wirfs-Brock

Today, the technology and tools of software development has achieved global ubiquity. Open source tools are available to everyone and we pretty much all use GitHub and educate ourselves via StackOverflow. Many of us work on distributed projects where we may not even be aware of exactly where in the world some of our colleagues live. Yet, software developers are still people and we live and work surrounded by other people who create a culture that influences us. The local tech culture may no longer significantly influence the tools we use, but it still influences how we work and play. This isn't just about east coast/west coast differences, or a Europe/North America/Asia differences. For example, there are quite significant differences between the San Francisco Bay area, Portland, and Seattle in how software developers approach work and many developers choose where they live and work based upon these differences. Location is important not because in influences the tools we use, but because it impacts the psyche we bring to work.

ALLEN WIRFS-BROCK is a Mozilla Research Fellow and currently spends most of his time working on evolving the JavaScript programming language and the future of application development. He is project editor for ECMA-262, the JavaScript standard language specification and is currently working on finishing the next edition. He was a pioneering implementer of object-oriented languages and, as a technical and entrepreneurial leader, helped drive the emergence of object-oriented programming as a mainstream technology.

Privacy and Security in a Networked World

Steven Fraser

Independent Consultant
Research Relations & Tech Transfer

sdfraser@acm.org

Djenana Campara

CEO and Co-Founder
KDM Analytics

djenana@kdmanalytics.com

Michael C. Fanning

Principal Security Development Lead
Microsoft

Michael.Fanning@microsoft.com

Gary McGraw

CTO
Cigital

gem@cigital.com

Kevin Sullivan

Associate Professor
University of Virginia

sullivan.kevinj@gmail.com

Abstract

As news stories continue to demonstrate, ensuring adequate security and privacy in a networked "always on" world is a challenge; and while open source software can mitigate problems, it is not a panacea. This panel will bring together experts from industry and academia to debate, discuss, and offer opinions – questions might include:

- What are the "costs" of "good enough" security and privacy on developers and customers?
- What is the appropriate trade-off between the price to provide security and the cost of poor security?
- How can the consequences of poor design and implementation be managed?
- Can systems be enabled to fail "security-safe"?
- What are the trade-offs for increased adoption of privacy and security best practices?
- How can the "costs" of privacy and security – both tangible and intangible – be reduced?

Categories and Subject Descriptors

K.4.1   Public Policy Issues
K.5   Legal Aspects of Computing
K.6.5   Security and Protection

General Terms   Policy, Privacy, Security.

Keywords   *Privacy, security, cost, design, soft issues*

1.   Steven Fraser

In Portland 2014, we return to a theme first discussed as a panel at OOPSLA 2008 in Nashville TN. At that time, we

SPLASH '14 Companion, Oct 20-24 2014, Portland, OR, USA
ACM 978-1-4503-3208-8/14/10.
http://dx.doi.org/10.1145/2660252.2661294

explored whether openness (many eyes) and transparency contribute to improved security and discussed the benefits of achieving privacy "and" security – rather than simply privacy "or" security. Has the state of the art changed for the better or is the combination of increasing system states and complexity leading to lose-lose trade-offs?

STEVEN FRASER is an independent consultant on innovation and technology transfer. From 2007 to 2013, Steven was the Director of the Cisco Research Center. His achievements included: increasing the visibility and leverage of Cisco-university research collaborations, fostering technology transfer from university research projects through the recruitment of PhD/Post-Docs, and accelerating internal technology transfer through the establishment of the Cisco Research Commons and the CTech Forum – a proprietary conference for Cisco Staff. Prior to joining Cisco, Steven was a Senior Staff member of Qualcomm's Learning Center in San Diego, leading software learning programs and creating the corporation's internal technical conference (the QTech Forum). Late in the last century, Steven held a variety of technology strategy roles at BNR/ Nortel including: Senior Manager (Disruptive Technology and Global External Research) and Advisor (Design Process Engineering). In 1994 he spent a year as a Visiting Scientist at the Software Engineering Institute (SEI) collaborating with the "Application of Software Models" project on the development of team-based domain analysis (software reuse) techniques. Steven is a Senior Member of the ACM and the IEEE.

2.   Djenana Campara

In the context of cyber systems, both attackers and defenders favor automated code analysis tools (dynamic and/or static) for detecting vulnerabilities. However, while attackers are satisfied with an *ad-hoc*, hit-and-miss vulnerability detection strategy, such an approach is not well suited for defenders, who need to be meticulously systematic in understanding the risks and designing security mechanisms.

A systematic cyber defense approach must go well beyond the knowledge of vulnerabilities. It needs to include a knowledge of the system, threats and risks to the system, safeguards and their effectiveness, and knowledge of the system's security assurance goals. Only when armed with this knowledge, can defenders assess and address the security posture of the system. While it is easy to claim that a system is *not* secure when at least one potential vulnerability is detected – to support a claim that the system *is* adequately secure for its operational intent requires a convincing argument and evidence. To provide the requisite evidence, vulnerability testing must be driven by a threat model that anticipates attacks and evaluates vulnerabilities.

Unfortunately, many of today's approaches to threat risk assessment rely on informal artifacts such as documentation and personnel interviews – making for a too subjective, non-comprehensive, non-repeatable approach that is prone to inaccuracies and assumptions about the true nature of the system risks and vulnerabilities. To create a systematic, formal, comprehensive and automated security assurance approach to validate that a system meets its security objectives requires the collaboration of multiple automated solutions from different vendors. My position is that the "magic glue" is a set of standards! Let's discuss approaches and results.

DJENANA CAMPARA has over 25 years progressive experience and leadership in Software and Security Engineering. Campara is the CEO and co-founder of KDM Analytics Inc. with expertise in the areas of: formal methods; formalization and information/data modeling; system and enterprise architecture; reverse engineering (binary and source); software and system security design and assessments; security assurance; network analysis; and developing technology strategies. Campara's expertise in design process automation led to the development of an innovative and time-saving security assurance and threat risk assessment tools used in industry today. Campara serves as a board member on the Object Management Group (OMG), an international standard body and co-chairs the OMG System Assurance Task Force. She also has served on the SAS Technical Advisory Panel of National Institute for Standards and Technology (NIST) and previously served as a Board Member of the Canadian Consortium of Software Engineering Research (CSER), an industry directed research program that creates a collaborative environment for industry, researchers, and students to stay competitive in the broader IT marketplace. In December 2010 Campara co-authored the book titled *System Assurance: Beyond Detecting Vulnerabilities*, which is used as a text by Master of Software Assurance course syllabus at Carnegie Mellon University.

3. Michael C. Fanning

Security is a quality measure of software often regarded as a necessary but secondary concern relative to the matter of extending program functionality in a useful way. The non-negotiable center of secure development (including effective security response) is a willing, informed and disciplined engineering process. The necessarily inconsistent realization of this goal can be offset by security-focused evolution of operating systems, runtimes, application frameworks, development tools and mechanisms for providing information to programmers. Inevitably, other critical properties (backwards compatibility, performance, interoperability, language expressiveness and engineer productivity) limit or actively work against security as a value. The answer to the question of what we should do is simple enough, 'that depends.' In an increasingly diverse, connected and decentralized software landscape, it's hard to imagine there will be a diminishing need for discernment.

MICHAEL C. FANNING is a Principal Security Development Lead on the Trustworthy Computing team at Microsoft. The bulk of his 20+ year career has been dedicated to development tools, with a particular focus on static analysis checkers. He was an original developer on Microsoft's .NET MSIL scanner (FxCop) and was development lead for the first release of this functionality (as well as C++ static analysis) in Visual Studio. Recently, Michael has focused on producing security-focused static and dynamic verification tools for web applications. He is a frequent collaborator in the tooling space across Microsoft and is listed on many related published or pending Microsoft patents.

4. Gary McGraw

Only ten years ago, the idea of building security in was brand new. Back then, if system architects and developers thought about security at all, they usually concentrated on the liberal application of magic crypto fairy dust. We have come a long way since then. Perhaps no segment of the security industry has evolved more in the last decade than the discipline of software security. Several things happened in the early part of the decade that set in motion a major shift in the way people build software: the release of my book *Building Secure Software*, the publication of Bill Gates's *Trustworthy Computing* memo, the publication of Lipner and Howard's *Writing Secure Code*, and a wave of high-profile attacks such as Code Red and Nimda that forced Microsoft, and ultimately other large software companies, to get religion about software security. Now, ten years later, Microsoft has made great strides in software security and building security in – and they're publishing their ideas in the form of the SDL. Right about in the middle of the last ten years (five years in) we all collectively realized that the way to approach software security was to integrate security practices that I term the "Touchpoints" into the software development lifecycle. Now, at the end of a decade of great progress in software security, we have a way of measuring software security initiatives called the BSIMM (http://bsimm.com).

As a discipline, software security has made great progress over the last decade. Of the many large-scale software security initiatives we are aware of, sixty-seven – all household names – are currently included in the BSIMM study. Those companies among the sixty-seven who graciously agreed to be identified include: Adobe, Aetna, Bank of America, Box, Capital One, Comerica Bank, EMC, Epsilon, F-Secure, Fannie Mae, Fidelity, Goldman Sachs, HSBC, Intel, Intuit, JPMorgan Chase & Co., Lender Processing Services Inc., Marks and Spencer, Mashery, McAfee, McKesson, Microsoft, NetSuite, Neustar, Nokia, Nokia Siemens Networks, PayPal, Pearson Learning Technologies, QUALCOMM, Rackspace, Salesforce, Sallie Mae, SAP, Sony Mobile, Standard Life, SWIFT, Symantec, Telecom Italia, Thomson Reuters, TomTom, Vanguard, Visa, VMware, Wells Fargo, and Zynga. The BSIMM was created by observing and analyzing real-world data from leading software security initiatives. The BSIMM can help you determine how your organization compares to other real software security initiatives and what steps can be taken to make your approach more effective. BSIMM is helping transform the field from an art into a measurable science.

GARY MCGRAW is the CTO of Cigital, Inc., a software security consulting firm with headquarters in the Washington, D.C. area and offices throughout the world. He is a globally recognized authority on software security and the author of eight bestselling books on this topic. His titles include *Software Security*, *Exploiting Software*, *Building Secure Software*, *Java Security*, *Exploiting Online Games*, and 6 other books; and he is editor of the Addison-Wesley Software Security series. McGraw has also written over 100 peer-reviewed scientific publications, authors a monthly security column for SearchSecurity and Information Security Magazine, and is frequently quoted in the press. Besides serving as a strategic counsellor for top business and IT executives, Gary is on the Advisory Boards of Dasient (acquired by Twitter), Fortify Software (acquired by HP), Raven White, Max Financial, and Wall+Main. His dual PhD is in Cognitive Science and Computer Science from Indiana University where he serves on the Dean's Advisory Council for the School of Informatics. Gary served on the IEEE Computer Society Board of Governors and produces the monthly Silver Bullet Security Podcast for IEEE Security & Privacy magazine (syndicated by SearchSecurity).

5. Kevin Sullivan

Security means sustained, justifiable confidence in one's safety from unacceptable harm or loss (physical, economic, social, environmental). Such security is an emergent and evolving property of a complex, socio-technical system within a complex and evolving socio-technical environment.

While faults in software are a crucial proximate cause of many security failures (and potential causes of even more frightening future failures), the deeper causes are often rooted in larger failures at the overall systems level to manage possibilities for unacceptable loss. Traditional systems engineers have the system-wide perspectives needed to address security as an emergent property, but they all too often lack the software expertise needed to manage threats posed by software. Software engineers have traditionally acted as systems engineers for mostly-software systems, but they are often focused at the code level, and lack the broader perspective needed to deal with phenomena ranging from software to regulatory, operational, human, and social phenomena. The cyber-security research community has traditionally focused on the mathematics of information and on reactive response to specific threats and vulnerabilities, but not so much on software engineering, human, or systems-level aspects of security. No established discipline is configured to address the problem we face now, as we enter an era of organically complex cyber-physical-social systems. Moreover, the extant research and practitioner communities exhibit "architectural mismatches" that can make it hard for them to work together. If we wish to be secure, then we need to rethink and significantly restructure our approaches to systems-level engineering of the complex systems of the future.

KEVIN SULLIVAN received his Ph.D. in Computer Science from the University of Washington in Seattle, Washington in 1994. He joined the University of Virginia as Assistant Professor of Computer Science. He received an NSF Career Award in 1995, the (first) ACM Computer Science Professor of the Year Award from undergraduate students in 1998, a University Teaching Fellowship in 1999, the Harold Morton Jr. Teaching Prize in 2000, and a Virginia Engineering Foundation Endowed Faculty Fellowship in 2003. Kevin's research addresses systems-level, value-driven software and systems engineering with a focus on non-functional system properties, trade-offs, and the satisfaction of diverse stakeholder value propositions. His current research is funded by the National Science Foundation, the Systems Engineering Research Center, and a U.S. Department of Defense Science of Security Lablet. He has also served as a visiting scientist, consultant, and member of the external technical advisory group for the Carnegie Mellon Software Engineering Institute. His current service activities include serving as Steering Committee Chair of Onward!, on the steering committees of SPLASH and AOSD, and as a co-organizer of several research agenda-settings and community-building meetings in the area of national-scale health information systems. In the fall of 2014, he will teach an advanced undergraduate course on functional programming and constructive logic.

Welcome Message from the SRC Chairs

OCTOBER 19–24

SPLASH

PORTLAND 2014

It is our great pleasure to welcome you to Indianapolis and the 2014 OOPSLA Student Research Competition! This year's SRC continues the tradition of allowing both graduate and undergraduate students to present their ongoing work and get productive feedback on their latest results.

We were very pleased with the overall quality of this year's SRC entries. The SRC judging committee accepted 10 abstracts whose topics comprise program analysis, type systems, software engineering, parallelization, and program synthesis. As in previous years, the SRC participants will get a chance to give both poster and oral presentations about their work during the main SPLASH conference, and selected students will receive prizes and get a chance to compete at the ACM Student Research Competition Grand Finals!

We are very happy that you are able to join us for this exciting event, and we sincerely hope that participants get constructive feedback on their ongoing work at this year's student research competition.

Isil Dillig
University of Texas at Austin

Sam Guyer
Tufts University

Welcome Message from the Posters Chairs

OCTOBER 19–24

SPLASH

PORTLAND 2014

It is our great pleasure to welcome you to the SPLASH 2014 Posters session! This session provides an excellent forum for authors to present their recent or ongoing projects in a highly interactive setting, and receive feedback from the community. It is held early in the conference, to promote continued discussion among interested parties.

This year's Posters session includes both independent poster presentations and posters on papers that were accepted to SPLASH 2014 conferences, workshops, student research competition and doctoral symposium. We hope that all of these posters lead to many interesting and lively discussions. On the following pages, you will find the extended abstracts for the independent poster presentations, which cover a wide range of exciting topics in programming, systems, languages and applications.

We would like to thank all Posters authors and attendees for their participation. We would also like to extend special thanks to the Posters committee, Jeff Huang (Texas A&M University) and Heming Cui (Columbia University), for helping review the submissions and offering valuable feedback to the authors.

K. R. Jayaram
Poster Committee Co-chair
IBM T. J. Watson Research Center, NY, USA

William N. Sumner
Poster Committee Co-chair
Simon Fraser University, BC, Canada

Searching for Answers:

An Exploratory Study of the Formation, Use, and Impact of Queries During Debugging

Brian P. Eddy and Jonathan Corley

Department of Computer Science
The University of Alabama
(bpeddy, corle001)@ua.edu

Abstract

This paper presents the results of an exploratory study investigating the formation, use, and impact of queries during debugging tasks. The results of this study provide additional evidence regarding the impact of query-based debuggers and can inform efforts that are focused on developing and improving query-based debuggers.

1. Introduction

Query-based debugging (QBD) provides query languages to developers that facilitate asking questions about a program [3]. QBD tools must provide some range of available query types. This leads to the question "what types of queries are most important to support"? Previous researchers have approached this question. Sillito et al. present a set of 44 generic queries drawn from an exploratory study [4]. The 44 queries are categorized based on when the query was posed during the mental model building process. LaToza et al. presented a detailed analysis of a single type of query which they termed reachability questions [1]. A reachability question was defined as a query searching across all possible paths of execution. Collectively, these works have identified query types and discussed in depth a single query type. However, we identify a new set of query types based upon the type of information each query is seeking. These types can be seen as complimentary to existing work in further examining and categorizing the types of queries developers utilize during a debugging task.

This paper describes a study that investigated how developers form and use queries without formal query-based debugging support. The study explored the types of queries formed without formal query support in order to prevent any bias introduced by a specific formal query language. We also sought to understand how successful queries impact task completion during a debugging session. During study, we discovered initial results and insights that can aid in the development of improved query-based debugging systems. There were two primary research questions that guided this study. RQ1: Do queries significantly impact debugging? RQ2: What types of queries are used by developers?

2. Exploratory Study of Queries

We collected results from eight graduate students in computer science at the University of Alabama. Subjects ranged from 1 year to 10 years of experience in Java development with an average of 5.4 years of Java experience and an average of 5 years experience in Eclipse. On average, each subject previously completed 16.75 projects in Java in a professional or academic environment (15.3 projects in the Eclipse IDE). Of these projects, four of the subjects reported an average project size greater than 10,000 lines of code.

Subjects were asked to assume the role of a new developer for Apache Ant. For two distinct bugs (IDs 38175 and 38082), the goal was to identify all relevant portions of the source code and perform any necessary modifications to the system. The two bug reports provided to the subjects were retrieved from the Apache Bugzilla repository [1].

Subjects scheduled a time to perform the debugging tasks. Subjects were given instructions for completing the debugging tasks. The subjects were provided a computer with Eclipse v4.2 installed. The source code for Apache ANT and two runtime configurations designed to test the bugs were preloaded. We selected Apache Ant (v1.6.5, rev 367135) as the subject system based on size and domain. Additionally, subjects were provided with the ANT documentation and Java SE7 javadocs. A screen capture application was setup to run during the experiment. Subjects were informed of the screen capture software monitoring their us-

SPLASH '14,   October 20–24, 2014, Portland, OR, USA.
Copyright is held by the owner/author(s).
ACM 978-1-4503-3208-8/14/10.
http://dx.doi.org/10.1145/2660252.2660392

---

[1] https://issues.apache.org/bugzilla/

age. Subjects were instructed in the think-aloud method [2] that was required during the study. The think-aloud method requires subjects to explain verbally their internal processes that are not otherwise observable. Upon completing the task or reaching 1 hour of elapsed time, the subjects were asked to complete a post-survey for each task to rank perceived difficulty, frustration, effort, as well as briefly describe the process used to complete or attempt the task.

We reviewed the screen captures and collected the results into a data collection form. Using the collection form, we recorded instances of queries. Queries were either directly expressed or implied. An implied query was identified through developer actions (e.g., using a print statement to determine a variable's state). The implied queries represent queries that might be expressed by developers given the proper query language or tools. To avoid misinterpreting participants, we reviewed the recorded sessions independently.

3. Results of Exploratory Study

3.1 Do queries significantly impact debugging?

Six subjects worked on both tasks and all subjects worked on task 1. Some subjects never attempted task 2. For task 1, the minimum number of queries formed was 7, the maximum was 32, with a mean of 16.75 and a standard deviation of 7.96. For task 2, the minimum number of queries formed by a subject that started the task was 2, the maximum was 16, with a mean of 5.67 and a standard deviation of 5.24. A subject formed at least 2 queries for any attempted task.

We computed the query satisfaction rates for each subject on both tasks by dividing the satisfied queries by the total number of queries. The results of these calculations were then compared. In most cases, the rates for successful tasks are higher than the rates for unsuccessful tasks. We performed a one-tailed Wilcoxon rank sum test to determine if this difference was significant. With $p<.05$, we confirmed the rates are significantly higher for successful tasks.

3.2 What types of queries are used by developers?

We used a grounded theory approach to identify the query types. We analyzed the type of information each query was seeking. We identified two major categories of queries (*Document* and *Design*). The *Document* category focuses on locating portions of the source by treating the source as a set of documents. The *Design* category seeks to better understand the system by examining design-oriented aspects.

These two major categories were decomposed into five query types: *Text*, *Structure Behavior*, *Concept*, and *Responsibility*. *Text* queries (67 uniquely identified) are intended to locate text in the source code; an example is a query intended to locate parts of an error message in the source code. *Structure* queries (29 uniquely identified) are intended

to locate a portion of the source code based on a structural link such as where a method is called. *Behavior* queries (27 uniquely identified) are intended to ascertain how a specific portion of the source code behaves at runtime; "What happens in openSession?" is one example. *Concept* queries (17 uniquely identified) target source elements related to human-oriented concepts about the source code (e.g., parsing or copying); an example is, "How does the program handle parsing?" *Responsibility* queries (29 uniquely identified) are similar to concept queries. However, these queries ask what is the purpose of a source element or what concepts are related to a source element instead of where does a concept occur. An example is, "What is the purpose of Copy.java?"

4. Discussion of Study Results

The results of RQ1 indicate that each of the subjects, formed multiple queries for each task attempted. This seems to confirm that developers form queries during software maintenance tasks. Additionally, the results indicate the higher query satisfaction may be an important factor in successful task completion. Lower query satisfaction correlated with higher task completion. One possible reasoning could be differences in experience between developers. However, two of the more experienced subjects were present in the group that did not complete the tasks. Furthermore, queries that were not satisfied took time away from completing the task.

RQ2 focused on the types of queries asked by the subjects. The type that occured most was the text query. This query type occured more than the next two most numerous query types combined. However, our observations revealed that text queries were commonly sub-queries to another query type. For instance, one subject sought to identify where an error message was generated. This query lead to 8 subsequent text queries seeking occurences of the error message. With proper tool support, the number of text queries should decrease. In future work, we will seek to identify any existing tool support for each of the query types and which query types require additional support.

References

[1] T. D. LaToza and B. A. Myers. Developers ask reachability questions. In *Proceedings of the 32Nd ACM/IEEE International Conference on Software Engineering - Volume 1*, ICSE '10, pages 185–194, New York, NY, USA, 2010.

[2] J. Lawrance, C. Bogart, M. Burnett, R. Bellamy, K. Rector, and S.D. Fleming. How programmers debug, revisited: An information foraging theory perspective. *IEEE Transactions on Software Engineering*, 39(2):197–215, Feb 2013.

[3] R. Lencevicius, U. Hölzle, and A. K. Singh. Dynamic query-based debugging of object-oriented programs. *Automated Software Engineering*, 10:39–74, 2003.

[4] J. Sillito, G.C. Murphy, and K. De Volder. Asking and answering questions during a programming change task. *Software Engineering, IEEE Transactions on*, 34(4):434–451, July 2008.

HJ-Viz: A New Tool for Visualizing, Debugging and Optimizing Parallel Programs

Peter Elmers

Rice University

pe4@rice.edu

Hongyu Li

Rice University

hl33@rice.edu

Shams Imam

Rice University

shams@rice.edu

Vivek Sarkar

Rice University

vsarkar@rice.edu

1. Motivation

The proliferation of multicore processors warrants parallelism as the future of computing, increasing the demand to write parallel programs for increased application performance. Previous experience has shown that writing explicitly parallel programs is inherently more difficult than writing sequential programs. Programmers need parallel programming models, constructs, and tools that can simplify writing of parallel programs. In this poster, we present an innovative new tool, HJ-Viz, which generates interactive Computation Graphs (CGs) of parallel programs by analyzing event logs. The visual feedback is valuable for a programmer to efficiently optimize program logic and to eliminate the presence of potential bugs which may otherwise be difficult to detect. For example, in cases of deadlocks, HJ-Viz enables users to visualize and easily diagnose the deadlock scenario.

CGs provide an intuitive graphical view of a parallel program's execution. A CG is an acyclic graph that consists of: *a*) a set of nodes, where each node represents a step consisting of sequential computation, and *b*) a set of directed edges that represent ordering constraints among steps. A task can be partitioned into multiple steps, the key constraint is that a step should not contain any parallelism or synchronization.

We incorporate Abstract Execution Metrics (AEM) as well as Real Time Metrics (RTM) in the visualization. AEM describe the performance of a program by measuring the cost of abstract operations, such as floating-point, comparison, stencil, or data structure operations. RTM inserts timing calls to record the time elapsed between consecutive synchronization events.

Programmers can use the visualization of the CG by HJ-Viz to pinpoint potential sources of bugs and points of improvement for parallel performance. HJ-Viz highlights the program's critical paths and displays the amount of work performed in each step of computation based on the collected AEM or RTM. Our event logging infrastructure also maintains precise source code locations for each event, allowing HJ-Viz to display the code involved in the creation of every node in the CG.

2. Implementation

Our current implementation of HJ-Viz processes event logs produced by the HJlib runtime [5]. HJlib is an implementation of a pedagogic parallel programming model used at Rice University to teach a sophomore-level course titled "Fundamentals of Parallel Programming" [1]. Built on top of the Java Concurrency library [2], HJlib facilitates an effective learning process in topics like parallel patterns, thread safety and data race avoidance using a wide range of parallel constructs including async tasks, isolated, futures, data-driven tasks, phasers and actors [3]. HJ-Viz can be used to visualize HJlib programs written using **any** combinations of these constructs.

Usage of parallel constructs trigger events in the HJlib runtime which are used by the event logger to create the related entries in the event log. AEM data is also included when available. The event log is built incrementally and the complete event log becomes available upon program termination. This log is then processed offline by HJ-Viz to generate a dot representation of the CG. The dot file is then laid out and converted to a scalable vector graphic by Graphviz [4], and displayed in the user's browser with interactivity features implemented in JavaScript. Using web browsers as the renderer ensures cross-platform compatibility. As a result, HJ-Viz can be hosted on users' machines or on a central server over the Internet.

3. Visualization Examples

One of the goals of HJlib is to introduce students to the fundamentals of parallel programming. By providing visualizations for parallel programs, HJ-Viz makes it easier for students who have no prior experience in parallel programming to grasp the fundamental ideas in this field. Figure 1 shows a simple program written in HJlib that a student may come

SPLASH '14,   Oct 20-24 2014, Portland, OR, USA.

Copyright © 2014 ACM 978-1-4503-3208-8/14/10....

http://dx.doi.org/10.1145/2660252.2660395

across early on. This program deadlocks while using DDFs since the tasks at lines 4 and 5 are waiting on dependencies (B and A respectively) that are never satisfied unless their corresponding bodies are run. Having a visual representation of simple programs like these, as well as more complicated programs later on, helps in a student's understanding of the fundamental parallel constructs being employed. Figure 2 displays the CG rendered by HJ-Viz when this program is run. The two nodes with red borders highlight deadlocked tasks (as they are floating leaf nodes with missing join edges) which allows the user to obtain a better understanding of where the deadlock stems from. As seen in the figure, hovering over nodes displays the relevant source code snippet participating in the deadlock.

```
finish(() -> {
  HjDataDrivenFuture<Long> A = newDDF();
  HjDataDrivenFuture<Long> B = newDDF();
  asyncAwait(B, () -> A.put(B.get() + 3));
  asyncAwait(A, () -> B.put(A.get() + 5));
});
```

Figure 1: Deadlock with DDFs.

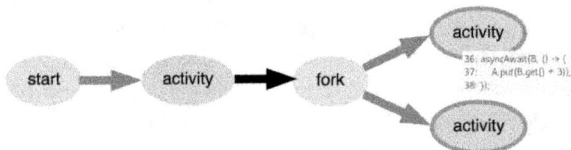

Figure 2: DDF deadlock CG.

Figure 3 shows a parallel MergeSort program. The CG in Figure 4 shows that under `finish` scope, there are two new activities being spawned by the main program. The two newly forked tasks work on different portions of the data with the same instructions. The two `finish` start nodes on the third level arise from the recursive call to MergeSort(), and in this case, each asynchronous call splits the list into two smaller parts, until the list is of unit length.

```
final int mid = M + (N - M) / 2;
finish(() -> {
  async(() -> mergesort(A, M, mid));
  async(() -> mergesort(A, mid + 1, N));
});
merge(A, M, mid, N);
```

Figure 3: MergeSort (merge code snippet omitted for brevity).

The CG can also be used to generate the parallelism profile of the program in terms of AEM or RTM. Depending on the number of participating nodes at each abstract work unit or real time interval in the CG, the chart shows how the degree of parallelism varies over time. Traversal of Figure 4 generates the bar chart shown in Figure 5. Users can write different variants of the same program (as shown using matrix multiplication in our accompanying poster) and

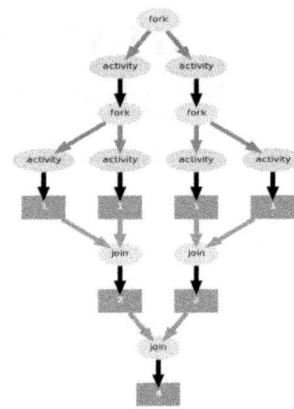

Figure 4: MergeSort CG on input array of size 4. The bold edges represent the critical path of the computation. Since all the edges are in bold, it means the computation is evenly load balanced.

generate the CGs and parallelism profiles for different parallel algorithms for the same problem. These visualizations are particularly useful when comparing the performance of the different algorithms and choosing the best performing parallel implementation.

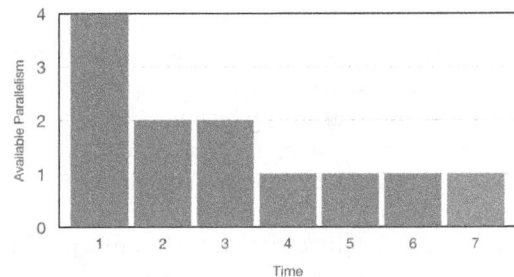

Figure 5: MergeSort available parallelism chart.

In summary, HJ-Viz renders the CG of a parallel program, providing an intuitive graphical view of the program's execution. The visual feedback allows a user to reason about performance problems and to optimize program logic to maximize available parallelism. The visualization also enables fixing bugs such as deadlocks which may otherwise be difficult to diagnose. As a result, HJ-Viz will be used at Rice University to teach a sophomore-level course in parallel programming. We plan to support visualizing nodes participating in data race bugs in HJ-Viz.

References

[1] COMP 322: Fundamentals of Parallel Programming. https://wiki.rice.edu/confluence/display/PARPROG/COMP322, 2014.

[2] Java Concurrency Utilities. http://docs.oracle.com/javase/8/docs/technotes/guides/concurrency/, 2014.

[3] V. Cavé, J. Zhao, Y. Guo, and V. Sarkar. Habanero-Java: the New Adventures of Old X10. In *PPPJ'11*, pages 51–61, 2011.

[4] E. R. Gansner and S. C. North. An open graph visualization system and its applications to software engineering. *Software - Practice and Experience*, 30(11):1203–1233, 2000.

[5] S. Imam and V. Sarkar. Habanero-Java Library: a Java 8 Framework for Multicore Programming. In *PPPJ'14*. 2014.

Detecting Design Similarity Patterns Using Program Execution Traces

Kuldeep Kumar
School of Computing
National University of Singapore, Singapore
kuldeep@comp.nus.edu.sg

Stan Jarzabek
School of Computing
National University of Singapore, Singapore
stan@comp.nus.edu.sg

Abstract

This paper aims at detecting an important type of design similarity patterns, so-called collaborative patterns, that has not been addressed in the software clone research so far. Collaborative patterns appear as recurring configurations of collaborating components such as methods or classes. Knowing location of such patterns and exact differences among them is useful in program understanding, better change impact analysis, code compaction, software maintenance, and in reuse. In the proposed approach for detecting collaborative patterns, we instrument the subject program with extra code to generate method execution traces. Then, we analyze generated traces to find collaborative patterns. Preliminary investigation has also been done to validate the proposed approach.

Categories and Subject Descriptors D.2.2 [**Software Engineering**]: Design Tools and Techniques, D.2.7 [**Software Engineering**]: Distribution, Maintenance, and Enhancement.

General Terms Algorithms, Design.

Keywords code clone; collaborative patterns; design concept; dynamic analysis

1. Introduction

Code clones are repeated program structures of considerable size and significant similarities among them. Detection of code clones can help programmers in reducing maintenance cost, in improving program understanding, and in controlling code changes. Many types of code clones such as simple clones—similar or identical code fragments [1], structural clones [2], logical clones [3], semantic clones [1], and their corresponding detection techniques are available in the literature. In this paper, we aim at detecting an important type of design similarity patterns that we call **collaborative patterns**.

> **Collaborative pattern** is a recurring configuration of program entities (e.g., classes or functions) inter-related by means of calling relationship (function calls or message passing). In these configurations, the corresponding entities should be similar to each other based on some selected similarity metrics such as textual, functional, structural, or logical similarities.

Collaborative patterns are large-granular clones. They result from applying standardized solutions and/or from recurring problems that naturally arise in software analysis or design spaces. Their knowledge in the programs is essential in re-engineering for reuse as it allows the developers to assess the reuse potential, and identify specific component configurations that can be reused.

Example: Project Collaboration Environment (PCE) is a web application that supports project planning and execution. PCE modules manage information about Staff, Project, Product, and Task. Each PCE module implements the operations such as create, edit, delete, display, and save to manage their respective records. Figure 1 shows design of features CreateStaff, CreateProject, and CreateProduct. Boxes are PHP files implementing user interface (Level 1), business logic (Level 2), and database aspects (Level 3) of respective features. Boxes of the same shade are similar to each other (i.e. code clones), and arrows indicate calling relationships among PHP functions in the corresponding boxes. Recurring configurations of these PHP files shown in the Figure 1 form a collaborative pattern.

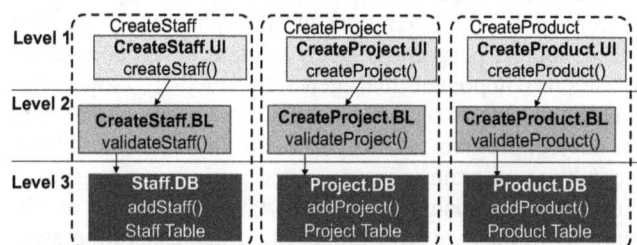

Figure 1. Three instances of a Collaborative Pattern in PCE

In this paper, an approach for detection of collaborative patterns based upon the usage of method execution traces has been proposed. The research contribution of the paper can be summarized as below:

1. Formalization of a new type of software clones i.e. the collaborative patterns (Section 2).
2. An approach for detecting the collaborative patterns (Section 3).
3. Design and development of a collaborative pattern detection tool for empirical evaluation of the proposed approach (Section 4).

2. Types of Collaborative Patterns

Consider six classes A, A', B, B', C, and C' with methods f(), f'(), g(), g'(), h(), and h'() respectively as shown in Figure 2(a). We refer to the method configurations <f(),g(),h()> and <f'(),g'(),h'()> as collaborative method patterns if we have method calls A.f()→B.g()→C.h() and A'.f()→B'.g()→C'.h(), where methods A.f() and A'.f(), B.g() and B'.g(), and C.h() and C'.h() are identified as code clones of each other (marked with same color in the figure). Further, if classes A and A', B and B', and C and C' are code clones of each other and collaborate with each other as shown by arrows in Figure 2(b), then, the configurations <A,B,C> and <A',B',C'> form collaborative class patterns. In the similar way, collaborative patterns can be defined at the level of files, directories etc.

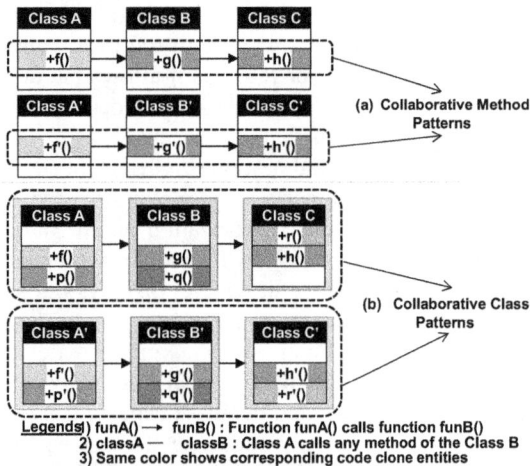

Figure 2. Possible types of collaborative Patterns

3. The Methodology

Figure 3 gives an overview of the collaborative pattern detection approach. It consists of four phases. In the first phase, subject program is given as input to the code clone detection component that generates method clones and class clones as the output. In addition, program structure of the subject program is also generated. In the second phase, the subject program is instrumented with the trace generation code to generate method execution traces at the runtime. In this, we have proposed a trace generation algorithm, RTTracer that captures only those method traces that have unique method execution sequence. Hence, the results of trace generation component are more concise and significant. We have developed a token-based string pattern matching algorithm, SMPR (Super Maximal Pattern Retrieval), that detects collaborative patterns using code

clones and program execution traces generated in the previous phase (phase 3). The proposed Collaborative Pattern Analyzer component (phase 4) helps in visualization and analysis of the collaborative patterns detected in the previous phase.

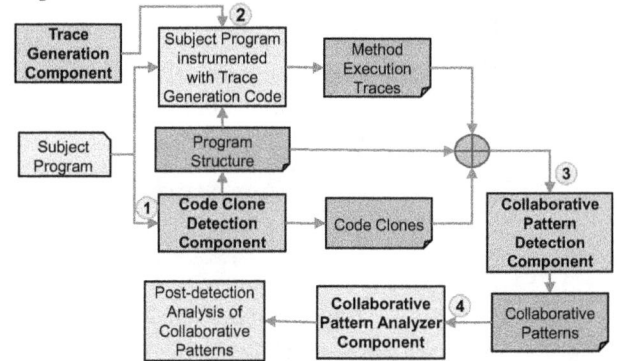

Figure 3. Collaborative Pattern Detection Approach

4. Tool Implementation and Evaluation

The proposed approach has been implemented as a tool that detects collaborative method patterns in the software systems. The tool has been implemented using AspectJ [4] and Java. The evaluation of the tool has been done on the Clone Analyzer Java project source code [5]. At present, the tool detects collaborative method patterns only from Java Classes. We plan to extend its support for other types and for other languages. The detailed evaluation of the approach is an ongoing work. We use it on public domain software in different application domains. Opinions of domain experts are critical in the final evaluations. Hence, a detailed industrial validation will be performed with active involvement of our industry partner ST Electronics.

5. Applications and Conclusion

The proposed work initiates a new direction of research in the area of software clone detection by allowing us to find a new type of software clones i.e. the collaborative patterns. Apart from the common benefits such as help in program understanding, reuse, plagiarism detection, software evolution, and maintenance, some of the other benefits that signify the impact of the proposed work are better change impact analysis, code compaction, and generics creation.

References

[1] D. Rattan, R. Bhatia, and M. Singh, "Software clone detection: A systematic review," Information and Software Technology, vol. 55, No. 7, pp. 1165–1199, 2013.
[2] H. A. Basit, and S. Jarzabek, "A data mining approach for detecting higher-level clones in software," IEEE Trans. Softw. Eng., vol. 35, pp. 497–514, 2009.
[3] Q. Wenyi, P. Xin, X. Zhenchang, S. Jarzabek, and Z. Wenyun, "Mining logical clones in software: revealing high-level business and programming rules," in Int. Conf. on Soft. Maintenance (ICSM), 2013, pp. 40–49.
[4] AspectJ, http://eclipse.org/aspectj/.
[5] Z. Yali, H. A. Basit, S. Jarzabek, A. Dang, and M. Low, "Query-based filtering and graphical view generation for clone analysis," in ICSM 2008, pp. 376–385.

Enhancing Conformance Checking for Contract-Based Programs

Alysson Milanez   Tiago Massoni   Rohit Gheyi

Department of Computing Systems – UFCG

alyssonfilgueira@copin.ufcg.edu.br,{massoni,rohit}@dsc.ufcg.edu.br

Abstract

In this work we present a test-based approach for detecting and categorizing nonconformances in contract-based programs, in specific for the Java Modeling Language (JML).

Categories and Subject Descriptors D.2.4 [*Software*]: Software Engineering—Software/Program Verification

Keywords contract-based programs; conformance checking; categorization

1. Introduction

Testing is commonly used to check conformance in contract-based programs, as verification by formal proofs is hard to scale and static analysis is, sometimes, limited for detecting general nonconformances. With contracts, early detection of nonconformances is highly desirable, as developers are able to provide a more reliable account of correctness and robustness of the software written [4]. Developers tend to apply automated, although incomplete, approaches, as verification by formal proofs is hard to scale. In the context of Java development, the Java Modeling Language (JML) [3] is a DBC-enabling notation (and corresponding toolset), with contracts as comments within Java code. For JML, there are basically two ways to automatically check conformance: statically, with tools such as ESC/Java2 [2]; and dynamically, with tools such as JET [1].

While static analysis tools can be useful for diagnosing a number of common errors (such as null dereferences and invalid accesses to arrays), they may be limited for detecting general nonconformances (those only arise in the runtime environment), furthermore they can produce false positives and false negatives. Test-based approaches present, on the other hand, lower costs and higher precision in detecting conformance problems. Nevertheless, those approaches present some limitations, mostly by falling short in providing (1) automatic test data generation; (2) unit tests that fully exercise sequences of calls to unveil subtle nonconformances (as seen in the example from Section 1.1); and (3) a classification for nonconformances.

1.1 Motivating Example

In this section, we present an example to illustrate the problem of conformance checking in a contract-based program. In JML, contracts are written as qualified comments (Listing 1). Visibility is omitted, for simplicity.

Listing 1. GenCounter class

```
class GenCounter {
  //@ invariant 0 <= cntGen && cntGen <= MAX;
  int cntGen, final static int MAX = 3;
  GenCounter() { cntGen= 1; }
  //@ ensures (b == true)==>(cntGen == \old(cntGen+1));
  void updateCount(boolean b){ if(b){ cntGen++; } }
  //@ ensures cntGen == 0;
  void resetCount(){ cntGen= 0; } }
```

`GenCounter` represents a piece of information about some named tag. This class has a constructor and two methods: one for updating and another for resetting values. JML method postconditions are declared with keyword `ensures`. The invariant clause must hold after constructor execution, and before and after every method call. The \old clause is used to refer to pre-state of a given variable.

Despite its supposed simplicity, the program in Listing 1 is not in conformance with the specified contracts, since `GenCounter`, when exercised with a sequence of at least three calls to update- Count with argument $m = true$ - this case is revealed by the test case in Listing 2. An additional precondition to `updateCount`, testing whether the value of `cntGen` does not exceed `MAX`, would have avoided this failure. Thus, an approach that automatically detects and suggests a likely cause for contract violations can be useful to software quality maintenance.

Listing 2. A test case that reveals the nonconformance

```
GenCounter g = new GenCounter(); g.updateCount(true);
g.updateCount(true); g.updateCount(true);
```

2. Solution

In this work, we propose and implement a RGT-based (Randomly-Generated Tests) approach to detect nonconformances, and heuristics for suggesting categorizations for those nonconformances. Our approach automatically generates and executes tests, comparing the test results with oracles (generated from the contracts). The generated tests are composed of sequences of calls to methods and constructors under test, while the test oracles are assertions from the contracts, generated from JML contracts by specialized compilers, such as *jmlc* and *OpenJML*. After test execution, two filters are applied: first, *meaningless* test cases are discarded [1]; they violate a precondition in the first call to a method under test. The remaining *failures* consist of relevant contract violations, which are candidate nonconformances. The second filter distinguishes faults from the returned failures – those faults make up the nonconformances subject to the process of automatic categorization.

Regarding nonconformance categorization, we propose a three-level model composed by a category, a type and a likely cause. The category corresponds to the artifact in which probably occurs the nonconformance – source code or contract. The type is given automatically by the assertion checker, and corresponds to the part of JML that was violated - considering only visible behavior from the systems. The suggested likely cause is given by specific heuristics derived from our experience in investigate likely causes for nonconformances. This model is implemented in a heuristics-based approach, which suggests a specific category and likely cause for a given nonconformance. Each heuristic is based on a set of possible scenarios related to the type of detected nonconformance. Based on the contract-based program, the nonconformance type and the corresponding set of heuristics; a likely cause is suggested. For example, regarding an invariant error, we suggest a likely cause with the following heuristics: (1) Assuming an invariant error in class C, check whether there are some fields in C not initialized into the constructor; in this case, suggest category *Code error*; (2) Otherwise, check whether there is the default precondition (*true*), or no precondition at all, or whether there is at least one field modified on the method body; in either case, the heuristics suggest category *Contract error*, and likely cause *Weak precondition*; (3) Otherwise, *Strong invariant* is the suggested likely cause.

From the example in Section 1.1 that presents an invariant violation, once the method `updateCount` does not have an explicit precondition (it receives the default *true*), the likely cause suggested is *Weak precondition*.

JMLOK 2.0[1] is the implementation of this approach in the context of Java/JML programs (JMLOK 2.0 is an improvement of JMLOK [5]). While JMLOK was able to generate tests and display the test results between *meaningless* and *relevant*; JMLOK 2.0 is able to detect and categorize nonconformances, showing only the distinct ones.

3. Evaluation

We evaluate our approach by means of three empirical studies. First we assess our detection approach and our manual categorization process in open-source contract-based programs. In this study, 84 nonconformances were detected, the majority related to *postcondition errors* with likely causes between *Weak preconditions* (mostly related to the lack of preconditions for the methods) and *Code errors* (mostly related to null fields). Second we compare our tool with JET; the JET tool unveiled 9 nonconformances with coverage of 56.97% Java instructions and 47.97% of JML coverage, while the JMLOK 2.0 tool detected 30 by covering 78.44% of Java and 67.67% of JML; on the same units. So, we found that the JMLOK 2.0 tool performs better for both criteria. Third, an implementation of the categorization model is evaluated with a module to JMLOK 2.0 in a single set of contract-based programs. We collect the ratio between the number of coincidences between manual and automatic categorization and the number of total categorized nonconformances. We found a value of 0.73. The full results are available on the project's web site.

4. Conclusions

In this work, we present an approach for detecting and categorizing nonconformances in contract-based programs. The results are promising for applying heuristics in the context of these programs, fostering a more widespread adoption of such methodology by lowering the costs of conformance checking. As future work, we intend to improve the test generation method for more efficient detection of nonconformances, in addition to better categorization heuristics.

Acknowledgments

This work was supported by CAPES and the National Institute of Science and Technology for Software Engineering (INES[2]), funded by CNPq, grant 573964/2008-4.

References

[1] Y. Cheon. Automated Random Testing to Detect Specification-Code Inconsistencies. In *SETP*, 2007.

[2] D. Cok and J. Kiniry. ESC/Java2: Uniting ESC/Java and JML – Progress and issues in building and using ESC/Java2. In *CASSIS*, 2004.

[3] G. Leavens, A. Baker, and C. Ruby. Preliminary Design of JML: A Behavioral Interface Specification Language for Java. *SIGSOFT Softw. Eng. Notes*, 31(3), 2006.

[4] B. Meyer. *Object-Oriented Software Construction*. Prentice Hall, 1997.

[5] C. Varjão, R. Gheyi, T. Massoni, and G. Soares. JMLOK: Uma Ferramenta para Verificar Conformidade em Programas Java/JML. In *CBSoft (Tools session)*, 2011.

---

[1] http://massoni.computacao.ufcg.edu.br/home/jmlok

[2] www.ines.org.br

Self-Adaptive Parallel Programming
Through Tunable Concurrency

Tai Nguyen   Xinghui Zhao

School of Engineering and Computer Science, Washington State University
{tai.t.nguyen, x.zhao}@wsu.edu

Abstract

Recent advances in hardware architectures, particularly multicore and manycore systems, implicitly require programmers to write concurrent programs. However, writing correct and efficient concurrent programs is challenging. We envision a system where the concurrent programs can be self-adaptive when executing on different hardware. We have developed two different tuning policies, which enable users' programs to adjust their level of concurrency at compile-time and run-time respectively.

Categories and Subject Descriptors   D.1.3 [*software*]: Programming Techniques—Concurrent Programming

General Terms   Performance, Experimentation

Keywords   Actors; Parallel Programming; Concurrency

1.   Introduction

Recent studies show that no matter how many cores there are in the processor, for most of the desktop applications, only 2 or 3 cores are more than adequate, and others are under-utilized [2]. The mismatch between users' programs and the underlying hardware presents challenges in leveraging the full power of the multicore technology. In this paper, we address these challenges by proposing a new parallel system that separates concurrency from the functionality code of a program. Specifically, we develop a tool which serves as a tune knob in between users' programs and the underlying hardware, by dynamically adjusting the thread-level concurrency based on different tuning policies. These tuning policies can be implemented separately from users' programs as plug-in modules at run-time.

SPLASH '14,   October 20–24, 2014, Portland, OR, USA.
Copyright is held by the owner/author(s).
ACM 978-1-4503-3208-8/14/10.
http://dx.doi.org/10.1145/2660252.2660394

2.   Tunable Concurrency

Our system is built on top of the Actor model of concurrency [1], because it provides a convenient and less error-prone way to write concurrent programs. The Actor model encapsulates objects along with threads of execution. Therefore, earlier actor frameworks usually use one-thread-per-actor implementation of actors. However, it turns out that in practice, one-thread-per-actor implementation of actors is not particularly efficient, because of the overhead caused by context-switching among actor threads. It is more efficient to have a pool of threads, where each thread processes messages for multiple actors in some order, as shown in the latest version of ActorFoundry [3]. This observation has led us to explore the potentials of programming with decoupled concurrency. In other words, the code of functionality can be separated from the code of concurrency. In ActorFoundry, a fixed number of worker threads are employed for processing messages for all actors, and this number does not change throughout the course of execution.[1] We investigate the opportunities to dynamically tune this number to change level of concurrency at run time based on different policies.

Static Tuning: Separating level of concurrency from users' programs enable us to tune the level of concurrency based on the hardware configuration. As shown in Figure 1(a), static tuning is a concurrency tuning policy which takes into consideration the underlying hardware configuration at the compile-time, and then makes decisions on the suitable level of concurrency for users' programs. Static tuning is performed at the compile-time, therefore it does not introduce run-time overhead which affects the applications' performance. However, static tuning requires that the information about the available hardware resources is known in advance, and the application can fully utilize the hardware resources, i.e., no other computations are competing for resources.

Dynamic Tuning: Figure 1(b) shows the dynamic tuning policy which should be enforced at the run-time. Specifically, the dynamic tuning policy initializes the thread pool by setting the number of worker threads to be a small number,

---

[1] Unless starvation happens, which violates the Actor model's fairness property, in that case more workers will be created in ActorFoundry.

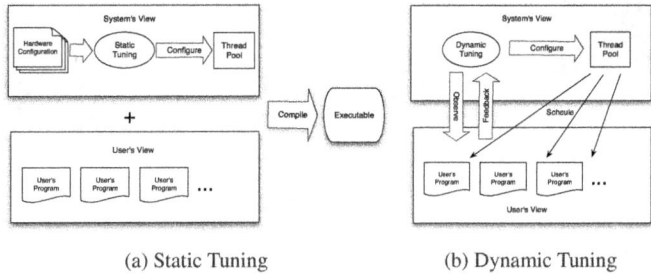

(a) Static Tuning   (b) Dynamic Tuning

Figure 1. Concurrency Tuning

i.e., 1. During run-time, it increases the number of worker threads, and observes the progress of the user' application. If the feedback is positive, which means increasing the number of worker threads results in better performance than before, the dynamic tuning increases the number of worker threads again, until the feedback from user's application becomes negative, which indicates that a balance has been reached. At this point, increasing the number of worker threads again usually results in negative impact on the overall performance, because of unnecessary context switching. Dynamic tuning can be invoked periodically with different tuning directions (increasing or decreasing), aiming for achieving better performance.

Dynamic tuning is different from static tuning in that it does not require prior knowledge about the available hardware resources. It is performed at run-time and adjusts the level of concurrency dynamically based on the progress of the user's application. Therefore, it is a feedback based approach, and it is more flexible in adapting to changes of resource availability in the system. However, it does require that the progress of application can be evaluated at run-time. For a large class of iteration based problems, such as scientific computing problems, the progress of application can be simply represented by the number of iterations that have been completed.

3. Experimental Results

We illustrate the effectiveness of our approach using a case study, Gravitational N-Body Problem (GNBP). We choose GNBP as an example, because it represents a large class of computations which consist of a series of parallel computations connected by barriers. We have implemented GNBP using manager-worker style. Specifically, a *manager* actor broadcasts a signal to the actors which represent the bodies. The *body* actors then read the information about all bodies, including their coordinates and masses, use the information to calculate the forces, velocities, and new coordinates for their corresponding bodies, and then send their updated information to the *manager*.

We run a 20000-body computation on both hardware for 200 iterations. The results are shown in Figure 2. In both

cases, our approach outperform the original ActorFoundry, and dynamic tuning achieves the best performance among the three.

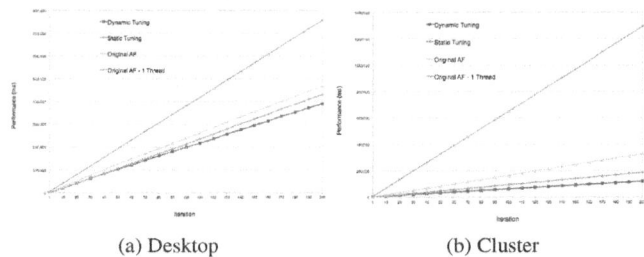

(a) Desktop   (b) Cluster

Figure 2. Performance Comparison of Tuning Policies

We have also carried out two other case studies, namely primitive root modulo N and matrix multiplication. All three case studies illustrate that with decoupled concurrency, we can bridge the gap between the hardware level and software level concurrency, and actively match these two for achieving better performance. Our approach does not result in extra overhead on the desktop, yet it outperforms the original ActorFoundry on the cluster node. Recall that ActorFoundry is already an optimized implementation of Actors, and its performance is much better than many other library based Actor implementations, and comes close to Erlang, which is known to be the most efficient language implementation of Actors [3].

4. Conclusion

In this paper, we present a parallel programming paradigm, in which concurrency is separated from the functionality code. Experimental results show that our approach enables users' programs to achieve optimal performance on different hardware without changing the code. Work is ongoing to apply the idea of concurrency tuning to non-actor based applications and data-intensive applications.

Acknowlegements

Support from the WSU New Faculty Seed Grant and the WSUV Research Mini Grant is gratefully acknowledged.

References

[1] G. A. Agha. *Actors: A Model of Concurrent Computation in Distributed Systems.* MIT Press, Cambridge, 1986.

[2] G. Blake, R. G. Dreslinski, T. Mudge, and K. Flautner. Evolution of Thread-level Parallelism in Desktop Applications. In *Proc. of the 37th Intl. Symp. on Computer Architecture*, pages 302–313, 2010.

[3] R. K. Karmani, A. Shali, and G. Agha. Actor frameworks for the JVM platform: A Comparative Analysis. In *Proc. of Intl. Conf. Principles and Practice of Programming in Java*, 2009.

Taming the Dynamic Behavior of JavaScript

Shiyi Wei and Barbara G. Ryder

Department of Computer Science, Virginia Tech
{wei, ryder}@cs.vt.edu

Abstract

JavaScript is widely used in Web applications because of its flexibility and dynamic characteristics. However, the latter (e.g., runtime code generation and dynamic object behavior) pose challenges for program understanding, security, etc. We have designed the JavaScript Blended Analysis Framework, a program analysis framework that combines dynamic and static analyses. *JSBAF* expands the capability of static analysis for the dynamically generated code and variadic functions. We also present a novel context-sensitive points-to analysis that more precisely models JavaScript objects. Empirical results on popular JavaScript websites show that our analyses are substantially more accurate than existing approaches.

Keywords   JavaScript; program analysis

1. Introduction

JavaScript is a dynamic programming language designed with flexible programming mechanisms, widely used in developing sophisticated software systems, especially client-side Web applications (i.e., websites). Its dynamic characteristics enable flexible and interactive features for the programs developed in JavaScript.

Unfortunately, the dynamism of JavaScript is a double-edged sword, posing software engineering challenges such as program understanding and security. Several constructs in JavaScript (e.g., *eval*) support dynamic code generation (i.e., generating executable code at runtime). These mechanisms provide opportunities for security exploits like cross-site scripting. JavaScript is dynamically typed and supports prototype-based inheritance. Furthermore, the properties of an object can be added, updated, or deleted at runtime so that a JavaScript object may exhibit different behaviors at different times during execution. This flexible object model poses challenges for understanding the behavior of JavaScript applications. Other JavaScript features such as function variadicity (i.e., a JavaScript function can be called without respecting the declared number of arguments) and constructor polymorphism (i.e., JavaScript objects created by the same constructor may have distinct properties), make function behavior unpredictable.

Given the ubiquity of JavaScript, it is crucial to build software tools that can handle these problems. The results of dataflow analysis enable tool building for optimization, assisting program understanding and/or detecting security vulnerabilities. However, the dynamic features of JavaScript render existing static analysis approaches ineffective in many cases. Dynamic code generation mechanisms make static analysis unsound because standard static analysis only analyzes source code that is visible without execution. It is difficult for static analysis to build accurate models of dynamically typed JavaScript objects. Also static analysis usually builds conservative models in the presence of function variadicity and polymorphic constructors approximating all possible behaviors, but compromising precision.

We have designed a general-purpose analysis framework (i.e., *JSBAF* [3]) and a novel algorithm (i.e., state-sensitive points-to analysis [4]) that handle JavaScript dynamic features to provide practical JavaScript tools for software development and maintenance. We have demonstrated that blended analysis is more scalable and accurate than static analysis when analyzing JavaScript websites and state-sensitive analysis is more precise than another good points-to analysis of JavaScript [2].

2. JavaScript Blended Analysis Framework

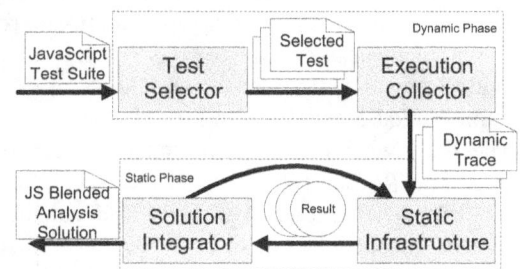

Figure 1. JavaScript Blended Analysis Framework

SPLASH '14,   October 20–24, 2014, Portland, OR, USA.
Copyright is held by the owner/author(s).
ACM 978-1-4503-3208-8/14/10.
http://dx.doi.org/10.1145/2660252.2660393

JSBAF is designed to judiciously combine dynamic and static analyses. It captures rich run-time information from JavaScript to account for the effects of dynamic features not seen by static analysis. Figure 1 shows the scenario of applying *JSBAF* for a JavaScript application. In the dynamic phase, the *Execution Selector* gathers run-time information (e.g., dynamically generated code, function calls and created objects) by executing tests selected by the *Test Selector*. The *Static Infrastructure* then analyzes the program represented by the dynamic traces with the Solution Integrator combining dataflow solutions from different traces into a solution.

In [3], we implemented an instance of *JSBAF* for finding the security vulnerabilities in JavaScript Web applications (i.e., blended taint analysis for JavaScript). The experimental results demonstrated the practicality of blended analysis, and its scalability and precision with respect to static analysis on 12 popular websites. Blended taint analysis was capable of identifying all 6 true security exploits that static analysis reported and found 7 additional true positives. Blended taint analysis eliminated 3 out of 4 false alarms reported by static analysis, leaving only one false positive. Moreover, blended analysis was more scalable, capable of analyzing *all* the webpages, while static analysis could not under a limited time budget. In [3] we also discussed actual cases for which blended analysis handled dynamic constructs with better accuracy than static analysis.

3. State-sensitive Points-to Analysis

Points-to analysis calculates the set of values a reference property or variable may have during execution. It is an enabling analysis for many software tools. In [4] we presented a novel points-to algorithm that can accurately model JavaScript objects. The analysis is partially flow-sensitive. Statements that may change object properties are tracked more accurately via a new control flow structure (i.e., *state-preserving block graph*), strongly updated when possible. An optimized property lookup algorithm is designed to more accurately model prototype-based inheritance. The analysis is also context-sensitive. We use a new form of object sensitivity [1] (i.e., state sensitivity). Rather than just using the abstract receiver object as a calling context in the analysis, we apply an approximation of the receiver object and its properties at the call site (i.e., *obj-ref state*). In addition, incorporating dynamic information collected at runtime, our points-to analysis can distinguish objects created by polymorphic constructors more accurately than a per-creation-site representation. Our analysis uses both the object creation site and observed local property names on construction.

We implemented a JavaScript reference analysis (*REF*) to evaluate the precision and performance of our points-to analysis. The *REF* client calculates the set of objects returned by property lookup at a property read statement or call statement. In our experiments, we use the term *Corr* to refer to the *REF* client based on a blended version of correlation tracking points-to analysis [2] and *CorrBSSS* to

Website	*Corr*			*CorrBSSS*		
	1	2-4	≥ 5	1	2-4	≥ 5
facebook	38%	52%	10%	50%	47%	3%
google	32%	51%	17%	53%	42%	5%
youtube	41%	47%	12%	54%	41%	5%
yahoo	48%	46%	6%	52%	45%	3%
wiki	29%	45%	26%	43%	39%	18%
amazon	45%	52%	3%	46%	51%	3%
twitter	32%	53%	15%	39%	49%	12%
blogspot	35%	34%	31%	53%	36%	11%
linkedin	34%	49%	17%	44%	50%	6%
msn	40%	36%	24%	48%	37%	15%
ebay	30%	40%	30%	46%	40%	14%
bing	41%	34%	25%	54%	37%	9%
Geom. Mean	**37%**	**44%**	**15%**	**48%**	**43%**	**7%**

Table 1. *REF* analysis precision.

refer to the *REF* client based on a blended version of our new points-to analysis.

Table 1 shows the *REF* client results for the 12 popular websites. Columns 2-4 present the results for *Corr* and columns 5-7 present the results for *CorrBSSS*. For each website, columns 2&5, 3&6, and 4&7 in Table 1 correspond to the percentage of property lookup statements that return 1 object, 2-4 objects, and more than 4 objects, respectively.

For *REF* analysis, the best result is that the property lookup returns only one object. On average over all the websites, *Corr* reported 37% of the property lookup statements were resolved to a single object, while *CorrBSSS* improved this metric to 48%, a significant improvement. In addition, *REF* analysis results may become too approximate to be useful if too many objects are returned. Although 15% of the statements on average returned more than 4 objects for *Corr*, *CorrBSSS* reduced that number to 7%. These improved precision results indicate the potential for greater practical use state-sensitive points-to information by client analyses.

Although our analysis incurred a 127% time overhead on average to achieve the increased precision, it was able to analyze each of the webpages in the benchmarks within the limited time budget, attesting to its scalability in practice. More detailed discussions of the experimental results were presented in [4].

References

[1] A. Milanova, A. Rountev and B. G. Ryder. Parameterized object sensitivity for points-to analysis for Java. TOSEM 14(1), Jan. 2005.

[2] M. Sridharan, J. Dolby, S. Chandra, M. Schäfer, and F. Tip. Correlation tracking for points-to analysis of JavaScript. ECOOP 2012.

[3] S. Wei and B. G. Ryder. Practical blended taint analysis for JavaScript. ISSTA 2013.

[4] S. Wei and B. G. Ryder. State-sensitive points-to analysis for the dynamic behavior of JavaScript objects. ECOOP 2014.

SPLASH 2014 Wavefront Chairs' Welcome

OCTOBER 19–24

SPLASH

PORTLAND 2014

Welcome to the SPLASH 2014 Wavefront track. Wavefront is a venue for connecting academic computer science research and current industry software practice, a forum to talk about how software technology affects our daily lives, and a community that seeks to apply the lessons learned in software development to improving best practices in industry and academia.

There are just a few Wavefront presentations this year, and a panel discussion we're very excited about. Our aim is for this track to stimulate discussion and build interest and participation for the future. We want you to be involved in Wavefront, bringing your experiences and ideas to the discussion. We invite you to think about how to apply some of the lessons from our speakers to your own development environment, and share those thoughts with us. Next year think about submitting a Wavefront paper, report, or panel!

Dave Archer
Wavefront Co-Chair
Galois, Inc.

Dennis Mancl
Wavefront Co-Chair
Alcatel-Lucent

Avoiding the Software Development Apocalypse through Continuous Build and Test

Eric Forsberg
Mentor Graphics Corporation
eric_forsberg@mentor.com

Abstract

Maintaining the stability and quality of a software product developed by a global team presents a myriad of challenges. A highly serialized build and test process turned out to be inefficient and in many cases detrimental to the health of the product. A system of integrated source control coupled with continuous build and test resulted in higher productivity by the engineering team, a dramatic reduction of "broken" builds, and a regression suite pass rate consistently near 100%. In this presentation we review the circumstances that motivated our move to a continuous build and test model, provide an overview of our continuous build and test system, and discuss the metrics used to monitor system health and drive continual improvements.

ACM Classification:

K.6.1 [Management of Computing and Information Systems]: Project and People Management.

Author Keywords: Continuous build and test; organizational learning; product release management

SPLASH'14, October 20–24, 2014, Portland, Oregon, USA.
ACM 978-1-4503-3208-8/14/10.
http://dx.doi.org/10.1145/2660252.266455

SPLASH 2014 Workshop Chairs' Welcome

It is our great pleasure to welcome you to Portland and the 2014 edition of the SPLASH Workshops!

Following its long-standing tradition, SPLASH 2014 will host 14 high-quality workshops, allowing their participants to meet and discuss research questions with peers, to mature new and exciting ideas, and to build up communities and start new collaborations. SPLASH workshops complement the main tracks of the conference and provide meetings in a smaller and more specialized setting. Workshops cultivate new ideas and concepts for the future, optionally recorded in formal proceedings. We invite you to explore the workshops program online at http://2014.splashcon.org/track/splash2014-workshops.

We were very pleased with the overall quality of this year's workshop proposals. We received 15 proposals and accepted 14 of them. To balance the requirement to meet the ACM Digital Library (DL) publication timeline as well as to provide workshop organizers sufficient time for preparation, SPLASH implemented a two-phase submission approach this year, with an early and a late phase. Workshops that wished to publish their proceedings in the ACM DL, had to choose the early phase. We are very grateful that our program committee supported this new scheme, even though it imposed a higher workload. We deeply appreciate our program committee member's commitment, making it possible to give thoughtful feedback on the received proposals and make decision in a timely manner. We thank all the PC members: Sophia Drossopoulou, Thomas Gross, David Grove, Robert Hirschfeld, Shan Lu, Indrajit Roy, Mario Wolczko, and Peng Wu.

Next, we introduce the accepted workshops.

Fourth Int. SIGPLAN Workshop on Programming based on Actors, Agents, and Decentralized Control (AGERE!): The AGERE! workshop focuses on programming systems, languages and applications based on actors, active/concurrent objects, agents and – more generally – high-level programming paradigms, promoting a mindset of decentralized control in solving problems and developing software.

Second Workshop on Domain-Specific Language Design and Implementation (DSLDI): The goal of the DSLDI workshop is to bring together researchers and practitioners interested in sharing ideas on how DSLs should be designed, implemented, supported by tools, and applied in realistic application contexts.

Domain-Specific Modeling workshop (DSM): An upward shift in abstraction leads to a corresponding increase in productivity. In domain-specific modeling (DSM), the models are constructed using concepts that represent things in the application domain, not concepts of a given programming language. This workshop brings together DSM researchers from industry and academia.

Foundations of Object-Oriented Languages (FOOL): The search for sound principles for object-oriented languages has given rise to much work during the past two decades. This workshop includes language semantics, type systems, memory models, program verification, formal calculi, concurrent and distributed languages, database languages, and language-based security issues.

The Future Programming Workshop: this workshop aims to build a community of researchers and practitioners exploring the frontiers of programming, in particular, it looks for new ideas that could radically improve the practice of programming.

Eclipse Technology eXchange (ETX): The Eclipse platform was originally designed for building an integrated development environment for object-oriented applications. The goal of the ETX workshop is to bring together researchers and practitioners to exchange ideas about potential new uses of Eclipse and how Eclipse technology can be leveraged, improved, and/or extended for research and education.

Mobile Development Lifecycle (MobileDeLi): The mobile domain presents new challenges to software engineering. This workshop aims at establishing a community of researchers and practitioners to share their work and lead further research in the mobile development area.

Fifth Workshop on Evaluation and Usability of Programming Languages and Tools (PLATEAU): Programming languages exist to enable programmers to develop software effectively. But how efficiently programmers can write software depends on the usability of the languages and tools that they develop with. The aim of this workshop is to discuss methods, metrics and techniques for evaluating the usability of languages and language tools.

Second Workshop on Programming for Mobile and Touch (PROMOTO): Today, new programming languages are emerging to enable programmers to develop software easily. PROMOTO brings together researchers who have been exploring new programming paradigms, embracing the new realities of always connected, touch-enabled mobile devices.

The First International Workshop on Privacy and Security in Programming (PSP): This workshop seeks to enable the development of safe software systems by getting the people of these currently isolated fields to start talking, working together and addressing this very difficult issue.

Reactive and Event-based Languages & Systems (REBLS): This workshop will gather researchers in reactive and event-based languages and systems. The goal of the workshop is to exchange new technical results and to define better the field by coming up with taxonomies and overviews of existing work.

Software Engineering for Parallel Systems (SEPS): The goal of the workshop is to present a stimulating environment where topics relevant to parallel software engineering can be discussed by software and languages researchers. The intention of the workshop is to initiate collaborations focused on solving challenges introduced by ongoing research in the parallel programming field.

Workshop on Technical Debt (TD): This workshop explores strategies for understanding the impact of technical debt. If we believe that technical debt is an important issue in long-term software product development, do we have ways to keep the technical debt from causing development gridlock? The workshop discusses some approaches to taking on technical debt from systems large and small.

Workshop on Stencil Computations (WOSC): Stencil computations describe an important computational pattern that appears in a large variety of applications, including image processing, physical simulation, and linear algebra solvers. This workshop aims to bring together these efforts along with users of stencils that require optimization to further the state of the art and promote a variety of research strategies for this important domain.

We are very happy that you are able to join us for this exciting event. Thank you for being part of this community, and once again, welcome!

Stephanie Balzer   **Du Li**
Workshop Co-Chair   *Workshop Co-Chair*
Carnegie Mellon University   *Carnegie Mellon University*

AGERE!

Programming based on Actors, Agents, and Decentralized Control

Carlos Varela

Rensselaer Polytechnic Institute,
USA

cvarela@cs.rpi.edu

Philipp Haller

Typesafe, Switzerland

philipp.haller@typesafe.com

Elisa Gonzalez Boix

Vrije Universiteit Brussel, Belgium

egonzale@vub.ac.be

Alessandro Ricci

University of Bologna, Italy

a.ricci@unibo.it

Abstract

The AGERE![1] workshop is aimed at focusing on programming systems, languages and applications based on actors, active/concurrent objects, agents and – more generally – high-level programming paradigms promoting a mindset of decentralized control in solving problems and developing software. The workshop is designed to cover both the theory and the practice of design and programming, bringing together researchers working on models, languages and technologies, and practitioners developing real-world systems and applications.

Categories and Subject Descriptors D.1.3 [*Programming Techniques*]: Concurrent Programming; D.3 [*Programming Languages*]; D.2 [*Software Engineering*]

Keywords actors, agent-oriented programming, asynchronous programming, concurrent programming, event-driven programming, decentralized control

Think Concurrent and Decentralized

Nowadays concurrency is part of every-day programming, including aspects that are directly or indirectly related, such as asynchronous/event-driven/reactive programming and distributed programming. On the one side, this calls for introducing fine-grained mechanisms, libraries and frameworks that make it possible to harness the power of concurrency in mainstream programming languages, and finally ease concurrent programming, which is a notoriously difficult task. On the other side, it is not only a matter of performance, but also of conceptual modeling and design, devising proper *abstractions* that allow for developing modular, extensible, reusable concurrent/distributed/reactive programs. Like never before, we need to investigate programming paradigms – either novel ones or those which have evolved from existing ones – that allow one to naturally *think concurrent*, and provide abstractions for modeling and programming a concurrent and distributed world.

To this purpose – following the successful path set in previous editions (2011, 2012, 2013) – AGERE! aims at being a premier forum to explore these issues taking actors/active/concurrent objects and agents – as well as any programming paradigm embracing a *decentralized mindset* [17] in solving problems and designing systems.

Actors, Agents and High-Level Abstractions

On the one side, actors and object-oriented concurrent programming [1–3, 10, 12, 13, 15, 19, 23, 24] unify object-oriented programming with concurrency, providing a clean and powerful computation model which is being increasingly adopted in languages, frameworks and libraries used in the mainstream. On the other side, agents and agent-oriented programming [5–7, 11, 16, 18, 21] – even if developed in the AI and Distributed AI contexts – provide a rich abstraction layer that could be effective to tackle the main complexities that concern the development of complex concurrent programs, featuring degrees of autonomy, proactivity, and reactivity. The objective of the workshop is then to promote the investigation of all the features that would make actor-based and agent-based programming approaches effective general-

---

[1] *ago, agis, egi, actum,* **agere**—latin verb meaning to act, to lead, to do, common root for actors and agents

SPLASH '14, October 20–24, 2014, Portland, OR, USA.
Copyright is held by the owner/author(s).
ACM 978-1-4503-3208-8/14/10.
http://dx.doi.org/10.1145/2660252.2662140

purpose tools for developing software systems as an evolution of the OO paradigm.

Besides, the workshop is meant to be a venue for all those approaches and paradigms that embrace concurrency in thinking and programming, providing proper abstractions to tackle important concerns, e.g. asynchronous programming, event-driven programming and the development of reactive systems [8, 9]. In particular, a relevant issue today – in particular in practice [22] – concerns the adoption of actors/agents/etc. together with other existing concurrency models, as well as with mainstream programming models and languages. So a main specific objective of the workshop this year will be to investigate – both at the theoretical and practical level – how to exploit actors/agents and related models/technologies with other reference approaches to concurrent/asynchronous programming, such as Software Transactional Memory [20], data-flow programming [14], and reactive programming [4].

Actors and Agents as a Software Development Paradigm

All stages of software development are considered interesting for the workshop, including requirements, modeling, formalization, prototyping, design, implementation, tooling, testing, and any other means of producing running software based on actors and agents as first-class abstractions. The scope of the workshop includes aspects that concern both the theory and the practice of design and programming using such paradigms, so as to bring together researchers working on models, languages and technologies, as well as practitioners using such technologies to develop real-world systems and applications.

References

[1] G. Agha. Concurrent object-oriented programming. *Commun. ACM*, 33:125–141, September 1990.

[2] G. Agha, P. Wegner, and A. Yonezawa, editors. *Research directions in concurrent object-oriented programming*. MIT Press, Cambridge, MA, USA, 1993.

[3] G. A. Agha, I. A. Mason, S. F. Smith, and C. L. Talcott. A foundation for actor computation. *J. Funct. Program.*, 7(1): 1–72, Jan. 1997.

[4] E. Bainomugisha, A. L. Carreton, T. v. Cutsem, S. Mostinckx, and W. d. Meuter. A survey on reactive programming. *ACM Comput. Surv.*, 45(4):52:1–52:34, Aug. 2013.

[5] R. Bordini, M. Dastani, J. Dix, and A. El Fallah Seghrouchni, editors. *Multi-Agent Programming Languages, Platforms and Applications - Volume 1*, 2005. Springer.

[6] R. Bordini, M. Dastani, J. Dix, and A. El Fallah Seghrouchni, editors. *Multi-Agent Programming Languages, Platforms and Applications - Volume 2*, 2009. Springer.

[7] R. H. Bordini, M. Dastani, J. Dix, and A. El Fallah Seghrouchni. Special issue on multi-agent programming. *Autonomous Agents and Multi-Agent Systems*, 23 (2), 2011.

[8] D. Harel and A. Pnueli. *On the development of reactive systems*, pages 477–498. Springer-Verlag New York, Inc., New York, NY, USA, 1985.

[9] D. Harel, A. Marron, and G. Weiss. Behavioral programming. *Commun. ACM*, 55(7):90–100, July 2012.

[10] C. Hewitt. Viewing control structures as patterns of passing messages. *Artificial Intelligence*, 8(3):323 – 364, 1977.

[11] N. R. Jennings. An agent-based approach for building complex software systems. *Commun. ACM*, 44(4):35–41, 2001.

[12] E. B. Johnsen and O. Owe. An asynchronous communication model for distributed concurrent objects. *Software & Systems Modeling*, 6(1):39–58, 2007.

[13] E. B. Johnsen, R. Hähnle, J. Schäfer, R. Schlatte, and M. Steffen. Abs: A core language for abstract behavioral specification. In *Formal Methods for Components and Objects*, volume 6957 of *LNCS*, pages 142–164. Springer, 2012.

[14] W. M. Johnston, J. R. P. Hanna, and R. J. Millar. Advances in dataflow programming languages. *ACM Computing Surveys*, 36(1):1–34, Mar. 2004. ISSN 0360-0300.

[15] M. Miller, E. Tribble, and J. Shapiro. Concurrency among strangers: programming in E as plan coordination. In *Trustworthy Global Computing*, volume 3705 of *LNCS*, pages 195–229. Springer Berlin / Heidelberg, 2005.

[16] J. J. Odell. Objects and agents compared. *Journal of Object Technology*, 1(1):41–53, 2002.

[17] M. Resnick. *Turtles, Termites and Traffic Jams. Explorations in Massively Parallel Microworlds*. MIT Press, 1994.

[18] A. Ricci and A. Santi. Designing a general-purpose programming language based on agent-oriented abstractions: The simpal project. In *Proceedings of the Compilation of the Co-located Workshops*, SPLASH '11 Workshops, pages 159–170, New York, NY, USA, 2011. ACM.

[19] J. Schäfer and A. Poetzsch-Heffter. JCoBox: generalizing active objects to concurrent components. In *Proc. of ECOOP'10*, pages 275–299, Berlin, Heidelberg, 2010. Springer-Verlag.

[20] N. Shavit and D. Touitou. Software transactional memory. In *PODC '95: Proceedings of the fourteenth annual ACM symposium on Principles of distributed computing*, pages 204–213, New York, NY, USA, 1995. ACM.

[21] Y. Shoham. Agent-oriented programming. *Artificial Intelligence*, 60(1):51–92, 1993.

[22] S. Tasharofi, P. Dinges, and R. Johnson. Why do scala developers mix the actor model with other concurrency models? In G. Castagna, editor, *ECOOP 2013*, volume 7920 of *LNCS*, pages 302–326. Springer, 2013.

[23] T. Van Cutsem, S. Mostinckx, E. Gonzalez Boix, J. Dedecker, and W. De Meuter. AmbientTalk: Object-oriented event-driven programming in mobile ad hoc networks. In *Proc. of SCCC '07*, pages 3–12, Washington, DC, USA, 2007. IEEE Computer Society.

[24] A. Yonezawa and M. Tokoro. *Object-oriented concurrent programming*. MIT Press series in computer systems. MIT Press, 1987.

DSLDI 2014: Second Workshop on Domain Specific Languages Design and Implementation

Sebastian Erdweg

TU Darmstadt
erdweg@informatik.tu-darmstadt.de

Adam Welc

Oracle Labs
adam.welc@oracle.com

Abstract

The Second Workshop on Domain Specific Languages Design and Implementation (DSLDI 2014) is collocated with SPLASH 2014 conference and held in Portland, Oregon, USA on October 20th 2014. The goal of the DSLDI workshop is to bring together researchers and practitioners interested in sharing ideas on how Domain Specific Languages (DSLs) should be designed, implemented, supported by tools, and applied in realistic application contexts. More generally, we are interested in building a community that can drive forward the development of modern DSLs.

Categories and Subject Descriptors   D.3 [*PROGRAMMING LANGUAGES*]

Keywords   DSLs, Programming Languages

1. Introduction

The Second Workshop on Domain Specific Languages Design and Implementation (DSLDI 2014) is collocated with SPLASH 2014 conference and held in Portland, Oregon, USA on October 20th 2014. The goal of the DSLDI workshop is to bring together researchers and practitioners interested in sharing ideas on how Domain Specific Languages (DSLs) should be designed, implemented, supported by tools, and applied in realistic application contexts. We are interested in discovering how already known domains such as graph processing or machine learning can be best supported by DSLs, but also in exploring new domains that could be targeted by DSLs. More generally, we are interested in building a community that can drive forward the development of modern DSLs.

2. Workshop Format and Scope

DSLDI is a single-day workshop consisting of a series of short talks whose main goal is to trigger exchange of opinion and discussions. DSLDI's topics of interest include, but are not limited to, the following ones:

- DSL implementation techniques, including compiler-level and runtime-level solutions

- utilization of domain knowledge for driving optimizations of DSL implementations

- utilizing DSLs for managing parallelism and hardware heterogeneity

- DSL performance and scalability studies

- DSL tools, such as DSL editors and editor plugins, debuggers, refactoring tools, etc.

- applications of DSLs to existing as well as emerging domains, for example graph processing, image processing, machine learning, analytics, robotics, etc.

- practitioners reports, for example descriptions of DSL deployment in a real-life production setting

All submissions, in the form of short abstracts (max. 2 pages) are subject to review by the members of DSLDI's Program Committee.

3. Program Committee

- Martin Erwig, Oregon State University, USA
- Matthew Flatt, University of Utah, USA
- Klaus Ostermann, University of Marburg, Germany
- Tiark Rompf, Purdue University and Oracle Labs, USA
- Tijs van der Storm, CWI, Netherlands
- Juha-Pekka Tolvanen, University of Jyväskylä/Metacase, Finland
- Emina Torlak, University of California, Berkeley, USA
- Laurence Tratt, King's College London, UK
- Markus Völter, Itemis/independent, Germany
- Guido Wachsmuth, TU Delft, Netherlands

4. Workshop Organizers

Sebastian Erdweg   Sebastian is post-doctoral researcher in the Software Technology Group at TU Darmstadt where he works on extensible programming languages and their application to DSLs. Besides DSLs, Sebastian's research focuses on static and dynamic analyses of program generators, language composition, type systems, expressive module systems, and formal methods. Sebastian co-organizes Dagstuhl Seminar 15062 on domain-specific languages (to take place Feb. 2015) and the workshop ParsingSLE (to take place Sep. 2014). He received degrees in Computer Science from TU Darmstadt (BSc 2007), Aarhus University (MSc 2009), and Philipps-Universitat Marburg (PhD 2013).

SPLASH '14,   October 20–24, 2014, Portland, OR, USA.
Copyright is held by the owner/author(s).
ACM 978-1-4503-3208-8/14/10.
http://dx.doi.org/10.1145/2660252.2663600

Adam Welc   Adam Welc is a Principal Member of Technical Staff at Oracle Labs where he works in the Virtual Machine Research Group. Previously he worked at Adobes Advanced Technology Lab and at Intels Programming Systems Lab. Adams general interests are in the area of programming language design and implementation, with specific interests in concurrency control, compiler and runtime system optimizations, as well as domain specific languages. Adam was the primary organizer of DSLDI 2013. He received his PhD in Computer Science from Purdue University in 2006.

DSM'14: The 14th Workshop on Domain-Specific Modeling

Jonathan Sprinkle

University of Arizona
ECE Department
1230 E. Speedway Blvd.
Tucson, AZ

sprinkle@ECE.Arizona.Edu

Matti Rossi

Aalto University School of Business
Runeberginkatu 22-24
FI-00100 Helsinki, Finland

Matti.Rossi@aalto.fi

Jeff Gray

University of Alabama
Department of Computer Science
Box 870290
Tuscaloosa, AL

gray@cs.ua.edu

Juha-Pekka Tolvanen

MetaCase
Ylistonmaentie 31
FI-40500 Jyvaskyla, Finland

jpt@metacase.com

Abstract

Domain-Specific Modeling (DSM) has proven to be a viable solution to the challenges related to abstraction mismatches between the problem and solution spaces. In many cases, DSM assists in the generation of final products from high-level models that are specific to a domain in terms of abstractions and representation. This automation is possible because both the language and generators are tailored for one domain. This paper introduces DSM and describes the related workshop at SPLASH 2014 (21 October 2014, Portland, Oregon).

Categories and Subject Descriptors D 3.2 [**Languages**]: Specialized application languages, very high-level languages; D 2.2 [**Design Tools and Techniques**]: *Computer-aided software engineering* (CASE)

Keywords Modeling Languages; Metamodeling; Domain-Specific Languages; Code Generation

1. Introduction

The primary drawback of most software and systems modeling tools is that they are constrained to work with a fixed notation. At the same time most users desire a customized modeling environment that can be easily tailored to contain the concepts needed in the user's problem domain. DSM languages (DSMLs) and tools provide viable solutions for making the development experience more flexible, faster and easier.

Industrial experiences of DSM consistently show it to be several times faster than current practices, including current UML-based implementations of MDA. As Booch et al. [1] state, "the full value of MDA is only achieved when the modeling concepts map directly to domain concepts rather than computer technology concepts." Accordingly, in DSM the models are constructed using concepts that represent things in the problem domain, not concepts of a given programming language. The modeling

SPLASH '14 Companion, Oct 20-24 2014, Portland, OR, USA
ACM 978-1-4503-3208-8/14/10.
http://dx.doi.org/10.1145/2660252.2662135

language follows the domain abstractions and semantics, allowing developers to perceive themselves as working directly with domain concepts. The models represent simultaneously the design, implementation and documentation of the system. In a number of cases, the final products can be generated automatically from these high-level specifications with domain-specific code generators. This automation is possible because of domain-specificity: both the modeling language and code generators correspond to the requirements of a narrow domain, often in a single company.

This paper introduces DSM by describing a general framework for defining domain-specific modeling languages and code generators for a specific purpose. This is followed by describing the focus and topics of the 14th workshop on Domain-Specific Modeling.

2. Defining and using DSMLs

Three things are necessary to achieve full automatic code generation from domain modeling: firstly, a modeling tool supporting a domain-specific modeling language; secondly, a code generator; and lastly, a domain-specific framework. Figure 1 shows these three elements at two levels: the definition level and the use level.

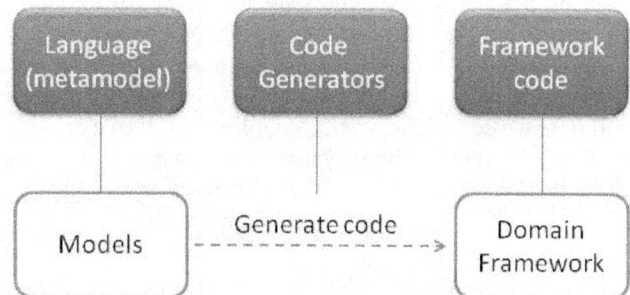

Figure 1. Framework for domain-specific modeling

The top-level (representing the definition) is made once by the organization for a given domain. Normally, one or two experts will define the modeling language (i.e., a metamodel) and related code generation, normally with a metamodeling tool [3, 5]. The metamodel is the implementation of the DSML, and includes the concepts and rules directly from the domain. The framework code will often be created by developers in earlier projects in the domain, with some being added or modified specifically for the DSM creation project.

The bottom-level process represents the use of a domain-specific modeling language and code generator. This level is performed many times, once for each product, by developers. Development time can often be further reduced by reusing parts of the model that are common to several products. The code generation and use of a domain framework or platform services require no effort by the developer. Together, these savings form the primary payback of the DSM approach amortized over each use.

This is unlike many visual modeling languages that are fixed to a specific notation that maps to semantically well-defined concepts of programming languages (like UML, SA/SD). With those languages, developers must leap straight from requirements into implementation concepts, and map back and forth between domain concepts, UML concepts, and program code. This requires significant time and resources, and can lead to errors.

In DSM, the specification models are built from instances of the domain concepts [4]. The code generator walks through the model and transforms the concept structures into code. In some cases, the code will be fully self-contained; more often, significant parts of the code will be calls to reusable components and the domain framework. Because the code is generated, syntax and logic errors do not normally occur, and the resultant improvement in quality forms a significant secondary payback of the DSM approach [2].

3. Workshop Focus and Topics

DSM has been successfully applied in many different domains. There are general characteristics about these domains that suggest useful DSM application scenarios. Each of these examples represents a type of configuration problem with numerous choices. Furthermore, each of these examples is based upon an underlying execution platform, or API, that may change. This makes a system brittle because of the tight coupling to the execution platform. Moreover, these systems are constantly evolving by virtue of changes in the hardware and software platform, and due to changes in requirements. Therefore, there is a need to incorporate several degrees of concern separation through higher levels of system representation.

The goals of the workshop are to collect and exchange experiences related to building and using DSM; continue building and extending the DSM community; and address in focus groups the issues raised in the presented papers and at previous workshops. The workshop examines DSM in different ways, including: 1) Full papers describing either practical or theoretical ideas; 2) Experience reports on applying DSM; 3) Position papers describing work in progress or an author's position regarding current DSM

practice; 4) DSM demonstrations describing a particular language, generator or tool.

The presentations of papers and demonstrations form the basis for discussion in the group work sessions. The results of the group work sessions, along with presentation slides, will be made available on the workshop website [6] together with the papers. The topics addressed in the workshop include:

- Industry/academic experience reports describing success/failure in implementing and using DSM
- Approaches to identify constructs for DSM languages
- Novel features in language workbenches/DSM tools
- Approaches to implement metamodel-based languages
- Metamodeling frameworks and languages
- Modularization technologies for DSM
- Novel approaches for code generation from DSM
- Issues of support/maintenance for DSM-based systems
- Evolution of languages along with their domain
- Organizational and process issues in DSM
- Demonstrations of working, or in-progress, DSM solutions (languages, generators, frameworks, tools)
- Identification of domains where DSM can be most productive in the future

References

[1] Booch, G., Brown, A., Iyengar, S., Rumbaugh, J., and Selic, B., *MDA Journal*, May 2004.

[2] Gray, J., Tolvanen, J.-P., Kelly, S. Gokhale, A., Neema, S., and Sprinkle, J,, "Domain-Specific Modeling," *CRC Handbook on Dynamic System Modeling*, (Paul Fishwick, ed.), CRC Press, 2007.

[3] Kelly, S., Rossi, M., and Tolvanen, J.-P., What is Needed in a MetaCASE Environment?, *Journal of Enterprise Modelling and Information Systems Architectures*, Vol 1., 1, 2005.

[4] Kelly, S., and Tolvanen, J-P, *Domain-Specific Modeling*, Wiley, 2008.

[5] Lédeczi, A., Bakay, A., Maroti, M., Völgyesi, P., Nordstrom, G., Sprinkle, J., and Karsai, G., Composing Domain-Specific Design Environments, *IEEE Computer*, November 2001.

[6] Workshop on Domain-Specific Modeling (DSM'14), http://www.dsmforum.org/events/DSM

ETX'14 – 2014 Workshop on Eclipse Technology eXchange

Jan S. Rellermeyer

IBM Research
rellermeyer@us.ibm.com

Tim Verbelen

Ghent University
tim.verbelen@intec.ugent.be

Abstract

The Eclipse platform was originally designed for building an integrated development environment for object-oriented applications. Over the years it has developed into a vibrant ecosystem of platforms, toolkits, libraries, modeling frameworks, and tools that support various languages and programming styles. The sixth ETX workshop provides a platform for researchers and practitioners to transfer knowledge about the Eclipse Platform and exchange new ideas. It is held in Portland, OR on October 21, 2014 and is co-located with SPLASH 2014.

Categories and Subject Descriptors D.2.0 [*Software Engineering*]: Programming Environments

Keywords Eclipse platform; integrated development environment

1. Introduction

The Eclipse project [6] started as a platform for building an integrated development environment for object-oriented applications. Over the years it has developed into a vibrant ecosystem of different platforms, toolkits, libraries, modeling frameworks, and tools that support various languages and programming styles. The project is managed by the not-for-profit Eclipse Foundation and driven by a large number of individual contributors as well as companies. Today, Eclipse is not only an important tool for building software, it is also a frequent subject to software engineering studies due to its large code base, bug tracking database, and due to having the largest coordinated release train in the open source ecosystem.

We are organizing a new edition of the Eclipse Technology eXchange (ETX) workshop format. ETX has been a very successful workshop at OOPSLA from 2003-2007 [1–5]. We feel that Eclipse is still very relevant in research and software engineering.

The goal of the ETX workshop is to bring together researchers and practitioners to exchange ideas about potential new uses of Eclipse and how Eclipse technology can be leveraged, improved, and/or extended for research and education. With this workshop we want to offer a platform to publish high quality scientific papers to show novel applications of Eclipse as well as novel technology that could become relevant for Eclipse.

The workshop will be organized as a one-day mini-conference and include the presentation of original papers on a number of topics related to the Eclipse platform as well as invited talks and a keynote.

2. Areas of Interest

Workshop topics include, but are not limited to, the use of Eclipse for:

- Integrated Development Environment (IDE)
- Supporting the software development process
- Debugging and testing
- Supporting design, requirements, and specifications
- Modeling environments and frameworks
- Aspect-oriented programming
- Program analysis and transformation
- Computer-based learning
- Software engineering education
- Teaching foundations of object-oriented programming
- Courseware
- Rich client application
- OSGi
- Applications on the Internet of Things
- Programming for an in the Cloud.
- Supporting the development of Android applications

SPLASH '14, October 20–24, 2014, Portland, OR, USA.
Copyright is held by the owner/author(s).
ACM 978-1-4503-3208-8/14/10.
http://dx.doi.org/10.1145/2660252.2662143

3. Workshop Organization

Organizers

Jan S. Rellermeyer (IBM Austin Research Lab, USA)
Jan is a researcher at IBM Research, an adjunct faculty at the University of Texas at Austin, and has been an Eclipse committer for many years. Furthermore, he has been an Invited Researcher of the OSGi Alliance, the standards group which develops the technology that the Eclipse platform is based on. Recently, Jan became the project lead of the Eclipse Concierge project and is actively working in the Eclipse IoT group. Jan's research interests revolve around systems and programming languages.

Tim Verbelen (iMinds - Ghent University, Belgium) Tim is a postdoctoral researcher at iMinds, Ghent University and his primary research interests revolve around programming support for real-time applications such as augmented reality on mobile devices. He has been using Eclipse technology in his research for a long time and recently became an Eclipse committer.

Program Committee

Werner Dietl, University of Waterloo, Canada

Didier Donsez, University of Grenoble, France

Michael Duller, Oracle Labs, USA

Michael Burke, Rice University, USA

Rüdiger Kapitza, TU Braunschweig, Germany

Miryung Kim, University of Texas at Austin, USA

Jan S. Rellermeyer, IBM Research, USA

Fabio Kon, University of Sao Paolo, Brazil

Martin Robillard, McGill University, Canada

Thomas Thüm, University of Magdeburg, Germany

Cesare Pautasso, University of Lugano, Switzerland

Tim Verbelen, Ghent University, Belgium

3.1 Review Process

We conducted a single-blind review process and every submitted paper received at least three reviews.
We would like to thank the PC committee members for their time and helpful contributions.

References

[1] M. G. Burke, editor. *Proceedings of the 2003 OOPSLA Workshop on Eclipse Technology eXchange, October 2003, Anaheim, CA, USA.* ACM, 2003.

[2] M. G. Burke, editor. *Proceedings of the 2004 OOPSLA workshop on Eclipse Technology eXchange, ETX 2004, Vancouver, British Columbia, Canada, October 24, 2004.* ACM, 2004.

[3] M. G. Burke, A. Orso, and M. P. Robillard, editors. *Proceedings of the 2006 OOPSLA workshop on Eclipse Technology eXchange, ETX 2006, Portland, Oregon, USA, October 22-23, 2006.* ACM, 2006.

[4] L.-T. Cheng, A. Orso, and M. P. Robillard, editors. *Proceedings of the 2007 OOPSLA workshop on Eclipse Technology eXchange, ETX 2007, Montreal, Quebec, Canada, October 21, 2007.* ACM, 2007.

[5] M.-A. D. Storey, M. G. Burke, L.-T. Cheng, and A. van der Hoek, editors. *Proceedings of the 2005 OOPSLA workshop on Eclipse Technology eXchange, ETX 2005, San Diego, California, USA, October 16-17, 2005.* ACM, 2005.

[6] The Eclipse Project. www.eclipse.org.

FPW14: Future Programming Workshop

Jonathan Edwards
MIT
edwards@csail.mit.edu

Richard P. Gabriel
IBM Research
rpg@dreamsongs.com

Alex Payne
Independent
al3x@al3x.net

Abstract

Visions of the future of programming, in the form of videos.

Categories and Subject Descriptors D.3.m [Programming Languages, Miscellaneous]

General Terms Future; programming

Keywords Programming; videos; demonstrations

The Future Programming Workshop gathers 15-minute videos that demonstrate a working prototype of a vision for the future of programming. The use of videos as a means of spreading ideas is starting to supplant traditional live demos and conference papers.

The purpose of the workshop is to explore and improve both the ideas contained in the videos and the videos themselves using the formal writers' workshop[1] method.

A program committee selected videos to be critiqued:

- Jeremy Ashkenas, New York Times
- Avi Bryant, Stripe
- Chas Emerick
- Steve Jenson

- Gregor Kiczales, U. British Columbia
- Andrew Ko, U. Washington
- Cristina Lopes, UC Irvine
- Sean McDirmid, Microsoft Research Beijing
- James Noble, Victoria U. Wellington
- Yoshiki Ohshima, Viewpoints Research Institute
- Roly Perera, U. Edinburgh
- Toby Schachman, Communications Design Group, SAP Labs
- Kevin Sullivan, U. Virginia
- Philip Wadler, U. Edinburgh
- Alessandro Warth, Communications Design Group ,SAP Labs

The output of the workshop will be the set of revised videos on a website to be announced.

References

[1]   Richard P. Gabriel, *Writers' Workshops and the Work of Making Things.* Addison-Wesley-Longman, New York, June 2002.

SPLASH '14 Companion, Oct 20–24 2014, Portland, OR, USA
ACM 978-1-4503-3208-8/14/10.
http://dx.doi.org/10.1145/2660252.2663601

MobileDeli'14 Workshop

Welcome Message of the Chairs

Aharon Abadi

IBM Research- Haifa

aharona@il.ibm.com

Danny Dig

Oregon State University

digd@eecs.oregonstate.edu

Eli Tilevich

Virginia Tech

tilevich@vt.edu

1. Workshop Overview

Mobile application usage and development is experiencing exponential growth. According to Gartner, by 2016 more than 300 billion applications will be downloaded annually. The mobile domain presents new challenges to software engineering. Mobile platforms are rapidly changing, including diverse capabilities as GPS, sensors, and input modes. Applications must be omni-channel and work on all platforms. Activated on mobile platforms, modern applications must be elastic and scale on demand according to the hardware abilities. Applications often need to support and use third-party services. Therefore, during development, security and authorization processes for the dataflow must be applied. Bring your own device (BYOD) policies bring new security data leaks challenges. Developing such applications requires suitable practices and tools e.g., architecture techniques that relate to the complexity at hand; improved refactoring tools for hybrid applications using dynamic languages and polyglot development and applications; and testing techniques for applications that run on different devices. This workshop aims at establishing a community of researchers and practitioners to share their work and lead further research in the mobile software engineering. The workshop has several goals. First, we want to develop relationships to create a vibrant research community in the area of mobile software development. Second, we want to identify the most important research problems for mobile software development.

We have two distinguished keynote speakers, invited talks, and research papers on mobile software engineering. We welcome you to work with us on these topics and define the next research directions in mobile software engineering.

Mobile software engineering presents new challenges and directions. Among others, we observe the following five areas of interest:

- **Management of the mobile applications**. This refers to the technical capabilities to create,deploy, and manage a suite of applications for multiple heterogeneous devices (e.g., iOS,Android, BlackBerry, Windows) that connect securely to enterprise back-end servers.

- **Hybrid applications versus native applications**. A native application is an application designed to run in a specific environment written in a specific language. A hybrid mobile application, however, is developed using web technologies such as HTML, CSS, and JavaScript activated by a native wrapper. Building native applications requires comprehensive knowledge in the specific environment, such as Objective C (iOS), Java (Android), and C# (Windows mobile and BlackBerry). However, hybrid applications based on web technologies require more common knowledge.

- **User experience**. Applications must be developed that provide different user experiences depending on the target environment. For example, an iOS application provides a different user experience than an Android application, even though the functionality of the application must be the same.

- **Battery life**. How can developers write software that uses up as little battery life as possible?

- **Migrations to mobile**. As more users access and use mobile-based tools, developers need to enable and support migration from legacy software such as web applications to mobile.

- **Mobile security**. Mobile devices has strong networking capabilities. Hence security of personal information and businesses data become very important. Employees use their smartphones to access sensitive information. The operating system of those devices collect sensitive data that may be visible to a third-party applications. Hence vulnerabilities from both the web browser and operating system must be considered.

Moreover, the development of mobile applications includes the following aspects that extend existing software engineering practices:

- **Software characteristics**. 1) Software is distributed on several platforms that link between them over the network. For example, one part of an application could be on mobile phones browsers, another part might be on the cloud, and both of them are reading data from some legacy systems. 2) Mobile applications need to be elastic and scale on demand according to their environments' abilities. Functionalities need to be easily removed, added, or moved to or from the cloud. 3) Many hardware platforms exist for an application and the platforms are rapidly changing, including flexible capabilities such as GPS, sensors, and input modes. Development, however, should be for all platforms.

- **Architecture**. Mobile application development also includes several architectural challenges, such as how to support omni-channel communications and how to support new application data updates from the server, e.g., notifications about new mail or software updates. Applications must be able to easily com-

SPLASH '14, October 20–24, 2014, Portland, OR, USA.
Copyright is held by the owner/author(s).
ACM 978-1-4503-3208-8/14/10.
http://dx.doi.org/10.1145/2660252.2662142

municate with new systems. Traditional solutions enable software to be easily designed and modified to communicate with new environments. However, the environments with which applications need to communicate are rapidly changing. As a result, traditional solutions do not fit modern software and we cannot modify applications using traditional architectural approaches to support all channels.

- **Testing**. Another aspect of mobile application development concerns software testing. How can applications be tested on arbitrary and unknown hardware? And how can we develop test-driven software without being able to run the test itself?

2. Organization committee, program committee

Organization Committee:

- Aharon Abadi, IBM Research- Haifa, Israel
- Danny Dig, Oregon State University, USA
- Eli Tilevich, Virginia Tech, USA

Program Committee

- Niranjan Tulpule, Google Inc.
- Luigi Pomante, University of L'Aquila
- Leonardo Mostarda, Middlesex University
- Bram Adams, MCIS, cole Polytechnique de Montral
- Anthony Wasserman, Carnegie Mellon Silicon Valley
- Shah Rukh Humayoun, University of Kaiserslautern
- Judith Bishop, Microsoft Research
- Emad Shihab, Rochester Institute of Technology
- Shahar Maoz, Tel-Aviv University
- Young-Woo Kwon, Virginia Tech
- Shmuel Tyszberowicz, Academic College Tel Aviv Yaffo
- Kate Farrahi, Idiap Research Institute
- Grace Lewis, Carnegie Mellon Software Engineering Institute
- Ashwin Baliga, Google
- Ran Ettinger, Ben-Gurion University of the Negev
- Omer Tripp, IBM
- Vinayak Naik, IIIT Delhi
- William G.J. Halfond, The University of Southern California
- Iulian Neamtiu, University of California, Riverside
- Komminist Weldemariam, Queen's University

2nd Workshop on Programming for Mobile and Touch: PROMOTO 2014

Summary

Judith Bishop

Microsoft Research
One Microsoft Way, Redmond,
WA 98052, USA
jbishop@microsoft.com

Arno Puder

Department of Computer Science
San Francisco State University
San Francisco, CA 94132
arno@sfsu.edu

Nikolai Tillmann

Microsoft Research
One Microsoft Way, Redmond,
WA 98052, USA
nikolait@microsoft.com

Abstract

Today, easy-to-use mobile devices like smartphones and tablets are becoming more prevalent than traditional PCs and laptops. New programming languages are emerging to enable programmers to develop software easily—leveraging the exciting advances in existing hardware, and providing abstractions that fit the capabilities of target platforms with multiple sensors, touch and cloud capabilities. PROMOTO brings together researchers who have been exploring new programming paradigms, embracing the new realities of always connected, touch-enabled mobile devices. PRO-MOTO 2014 would like to invite contributions covering technical aspects of cross-platform computing, cloud computing, social applications and security.

Categories and Subject Descriptors D.3.2 *Multiparadigm languages.* B.4.2 Input/Output Devices; C.2.1 Network Architecture and Design

General Terms Performance, Reliability, Experimentation, Security, Human Factors, Languages

Keywords touch-enabled devices; mobile programming; cross-platform computing; cloud computing; social applications; security.

1. Workshop Goals

The goals of the workshop are to discuss the issues surrounding touch and mobile programming and to plan future directions. The workshop will have papers, tool demonstrations and experience reports. The website for PROMOTO 2014 is http://research.microsoft.com/promoto2014/

Submissions for this event were invited in the general area

SPLASH '14 Companion, Oct 20-24 2014, Portland, OR, USA
ACM 978-1-4503-3208-8/14/10.
http://dx.doi.org/10.1145/2660252.2662136

of mobile and touch-oriented programming languages and programming environments, and teaching of programming for mobile devices. Topics of interest include:

- Mobile and touch-oriented programming languages
- Programming languages using innovative input mechanisms
- Programming environments on or for mobile devices
- Teaching of programming on or for mobile devices
- Programming tools such as debuggers on or for mobiles devices
- Libraries and programming frameworks that simplify programming for mobile devices
- Very large screens and very small screens
- Gestures, haptics and sound

2. Workshop submissions

The workshop received submissions from all over the world. Each paper was reviewed by three members of the program committee. The following have been accepted for presentation:

1. Jeffrey Schiller, Franklyn Turbak, Hal Abelson, Jose Dominguez, Andrew McKinney, Johanna Okerlund and Mark Friedman. *Live programming of mobile apps in App Inventor*
2. Thierry Renaux, Lode Hoste, Christophe Scholliers and Wolfgang De Meuter. *Software Engineering Principles in the Midas Gesture Specification Language*
3. Simon Baker, Stoyan Dekov, Fadi Fakih, Jan Medvesek, Venus Shum and Dean Mohamedally. *Supporting situated STEM learning - TouchDevelop Integration of the UCL Engduino over Bluetooth*
4. David Bau and Anthony Bau. *A Preview of Pencil Code*

5. Mohammad Reza Azadmanesh, Amanj Sherwany, Davide Eynard, Matej Vitasek and Matthias Hauswirth. *Mobile vs. Desktop Programming Projects: The Effect on Students*

6. Amruta Gokhale, Daeyoung Kim and Vinod Ganapathy. *Data-Driven Inference of API Mappings*

The selection shows an interest among the community in the engineering of mobile apps, of principles related to new devices, and in education.

3. Keynote

The keynote on "Programming gadgets with gadgets" will be presented by Jonathan de Halleux of Microsoft Research. Hardware 2.0 is upon us: cheap micro-controller boards like Arduino have gained massive adoption in recent years. Paired with 3D printers, cheap sensors and actuators, it allows anyone to prototype the next hot gadget. And yet, the maker will have to learn a soup of software language and framework to build a connected IoC solution: C++ for the micro-controller code, HTML + javascript for the client, some backend language and a communication layer to interact with the devices. In this session, we will show an attempt at unifying the compilation of web server code, rich client and embedded firmware under a simple mobile friendly language and IDE.

Jonathan 'Peli' de Halleux is a Principal Research Software Design Engineer in the Research in Software Engineering group at Microsoft Research in Redmond, USA, where he has been since October 2006 working on the TouchDevelop, Pex and CodeHunt projects. Peli has a passion for new technology and recently put smartphones in footballs to collect data in the cloud. From 2004 to 2006, he worked in the Common Language Runtime (CLR) as a Software Design Engineer in Test in charge of the Just In Time compiler. Before joining Microsoft, he earned a PhD in Applied Mathematics from the Catholic University of Louvain.

4. Organizers

Judith Bishop, Microsoft Research, Redmond, USA (General Chair and Primary contact person) – jbishop@microsoft.com

Judith Bishop is Director of Computer Science at Microsoft Research. Her expertise is in programming languages and patterns. She has co-authored a book on TouchDevelop, which is a mobile and touch-based language and IDE from Microsoft. She has recently been General Chair of the DDFP 2013 Workshop (POPL) and ICSE 2010. She has organised three Microsoft Faculty Summits. She runs the Microsoft Research ACM Student Research Competition. She has served on many program committees and is currently on the PC of MobileSOFT and SwSTE.

Nikolai Tillmann, Microsoft Research, Redmond, USA (Program co-chair) - nikolait@microsoft.com

He started the TouchDevelop project, which enables end-users to write programs on mobile devices. This project brings the excitement of the first programmable computers to mobile devices such as smartphones. Nikolai is currently on 7 PCs, notably CSTVA and ISSTA.

Arno Puder, San Francisco State University, (Program co-chair) – arno@sfsu.edu

Arno Puder is an Associate Professor at the San Francisco State University. He specializes on cross-platform tools for mobile app development. He is the founder of XMLVM, a byte code level cross-compiler that translates Android applications to other mobile platforms. Prior to his current position he worked for AT&T Labs Research on middleware related topics.

5. Previous workshop

PROMOTO started last year in Indianapolis [1]. It attracted 13 submissions and 27 attendees. The website and program can be seen here: http://pear.sfsu.edu/promoto2013/

6. Program Committee

- Hal Abelson, Massachusetts Institute of Technology, USA
- Tom Ball, Microsoft Research, USA
- Veronica Catete, University of North Carolina at Charlotte, USA
- Yael Dubinsky, IBM Research, Israel
- Matthias Hauswirth, University of Lugano, Switzerland
- Nigel Horspool, University of Victoria, Canada
- Chris Johnson, University of Wisconsin, Eau Claire, USA
- Suresh Lodha, University of California - Santa Cruz, USA
- Dean Mohamedally, University College, London, UK
- Michał Moskal, Microsoft Research, Redmond, USA
- Emerson Murphy-Hill, North Carolina State University, USA
- Vinayak Naik, Indraprastha Institue of Information Technology, India
- Wolfgang Slany, Graz University of Technology, Austria

7. References

[1] PRoMoTo 2013 proceedings, Judith Bishop, Nikolai Tillmann, Arno Puder, Vinayak Naik, arXiv:1309.5500 [cs.PL]

First International Workshop on Privacy and Security in Programming (PSP)

Tyrone Grandison

Proficiency Labs
Ashland, Oregon 97520
tgrandison@proficiencylabs.com

Michael Maximilien

IBM Cloud Labs
650 Harry Road, E3-418, San Jose, CA 95110
maxim@us.ibm.com

Raquel L. Hill

Indiana University
School of Informatics and Computing, 230E
Lindley Hall, Bloomington, IN 47406
ralhill@indiana.edu

Abstract

The importance of security and privacy in software engineering is now a pressing concern. Over the last decade, many programmers have recognized the importance of including security and privacy requirements at project start. This has led to efforts in secure/security engineering and privacy engineering, which focus on guidelines and best practices that can be used at the design stage to create safer code. Unfortunately, these disciplines are not pervasive and still in their infancy.

The goal of this workshop is to make security and privacy first class citizens in programming and programming languages. This forum aims to gather research and industry to further the discussion on how to 1) codify the principles from secure and privacy engineering into programming language constructs and or tools, 2) create programming languages that have security and privacy as foundational tenets, and 3) create/codify constructs or tools that enables secure and privacy-preserving (business) operations.

General Terms: Security, Human Factors, Standardization, Languages, Legal Aspects, Verification.

Keywords: Security, Privacy, Programming, Programming Languages

1. Themes, Goals and Format

The theme of this workshop is "embedding privacy and security into programming, programming languages, software and software engineering".

The development of secure software requires the specification and communication of functional and non-functional security and privacy requirements, the utilization of secure and privacy-preserving programming language constructs and the application of secure and privacy-preserving coding best practices. Currently, firms focused on developing code that is both secure and privacy-preserving will employ at most two of these techniques. Unfortunately, this leads to software with the appearance of being safe (i.e. secure and privacy-preserving code), but that offers very little real protection. You can have a secure design, but if there are no supporting language constructs then the systems won't be safe. If the programmer does not know the secure coding principles and is unaware of privacy engineering methodology, then the resulting software will not be safe. Additionally, privacy engineering is a relatively new area and researchers are trying to determine how to characterize privacy requirements. The specification of these requirements is an interdisciplinary undertaking; involving experts in law, business, and computer science.

By getting experts in requirements engineering, programming languages, formal methods, privacy engineering and secure coding into the same space, it is hoped that we can bridge the gap between the design and the implementation of safe code. This workshop seeks to enable the development of safe software systems by getting the people of these currently isolated fields to start talking, working together and addressing this very difficult issue.

The goal of this workshop is to make security and privacy first class citizens in programming (and programming languages). This forum aims to gather research and industry to further the discussion on how to 1) codify the principles from secure and privacy engineering into programming language constructs and or tools, 2) create programming languages that have security and privacy as foundational tenets, and 3) create/codify constructs or tools that enable secure and privacy-preserving (business) operations.

This is a day-long mini-conference, preferably on the second day of workshops. PSP will accept peer-reviewed submissions from the wider community and produce a proceedings that follows the ACM SIGPLAN-approved selection process and that is in accordance with ACM standards.

2. Organizers

The workshop organizers are:

1. Tyrone Grandison (CEO, Proficiency Labs)
Primary organizer and Contact Person
Mailing Address: Ashland, Oregon 97520
Email: tgrandison@gmail.com, tgrandison@proficiencylabs.com
Phone: 541-708-1191

SPLASH '14 Companion, Oct 20-24 2014, Portland, OR, USA
ACM 978-1-4503-3208-8/14/10.
http://dx.doi.org/10.1145/2660252.2662137

Background & Role: Dr Grandison leads an organization that specializes in supporting companies design, build and evaluate privacy and security solutions for their systems. He is active in the privacy and security spaces. He publishes and patents extensively in the field and serves on a number of panels and program committees. In 2014, he is the Program Chair for the Web 2.0 Security and Privacy workshop. He is also a Senior Member of the Institute of Electrical and Electronics Engineers (IEEE), a Fellow of the Healthcare Information and Management Systems Society (HIMSS), a Fellow of the British Computer Society (BCS) and a Distinguished Engineer of the Association of Computing Machinery (ACM). Tyrone will be responsible for assembling the Program Committee and managing the submission process.

2. Michael Maximilien (Chief Architect PaaS Innovation, IBM Cloud Labs)
Mailing Address: 650 Harry Rd, E3-418, San Jose, CA 95110
Email: maxim@us.ibm.com
Phone: 408-960-4761
Background & Role: Dr. Maximilien is currently leading the platform-as-a-service cloud labs at IBM Silicon Valley, where he is looking at how to make the CloudFoundry (CF) PaaS the de-facto standard open source PaaS. Part of this role is to look into making the CF cloud operating system one that is concerned with privacy and security for its users and operators. Max will be in charge of promotion and outreach.

3. Raquel Hill (Associate Professor, Indiana University)
Mailing Address: School of Informatics and Computing, 230E Lindley Hall, Bloomington, IN 47406
Email: ralhill@indiana.edu
Phone: 812-856-5807
Background & Role: Dr Hill is an Associate Professor of Computer Science in the School of Informatics and Computing. Her primary research interests are in the areas of security, trust and privacy for distributed computing environments and programming environments. Amongst other areas in this field, she has done research and published on incorporating non-functional security requirements into the design process and on using a domain specific language that provides information flow control to implement access control in Map-Reduce. Raquel will be in charge of the program.

3. Participant Preparation

Participants are invited to submit short and regular papers. Participants are also expected to 1) engage the panelists in the panel discussion, and 2) mingle and spark collaborations during the breaks.

4. Activities and Format

The workshop will go from 9am to 5pm. There will be one Keynote Speech that will last for an hour. The program will be filled with technical presentations and a panel discussion. Here is what we expect the schedule to look like:

9:00 – 9:15	Welcome and Introduction
9:15 – 10:15	Keynote Speech
10:15 – 10:30	Break
10:30 – 12:00	Technical Presentations
12:00 – 13:00	Lunch
13:00 – 14:45	Technical Presentations
14:45 - 15:00	Break
15:00 – 16:00	Panel Discussion
16:00 – 16:15	Break
16:15 – 17:00	Technical Presentations & Closing
17:00 onwards	Mingle…….

5. Post-workshop activities:

All the abstracts (and slides) for the accepted papers will be posted online. All the regular papers will be packaged into a formal proceedings and submitted to the ACM Digital Library.

6. References

1. M. D. Ernst. Type Annotation. http://types.cs.washington.edu/jsr308/.
2. S. Fink and J. Dolby. WALA, The T.J. Watson Libraries for Analysis. http://wala.sourceforge.net/.
3. M. Howard and D. LeBlanc. Writing Secure Code. Microsoft Press, 2001.
4. K.-C. Kang, S. G. Cohen, J. A. Hess, W. E. Novak, and A. S. Peterson. Feature-oriented domain analysis (FODA) feasibility study. Technical Report CMU/SEI-90-TR-21, 1990.
5. V. B. Livshits and M. S. Lam. Finding security vulnerabilities in java applications with static analysis. In Proceedings of the Usenix Security, 2005.
6. J. Newmsome and D. Song. Dynamic taint analysis for automatic detection, analysis, and signature generation of exploits on commodity software. In Proceedings of Network and Distributed System Security Symposium, 2005.
7. W. Xu, S. Hatkar, and R. Sekar. Taint-enhanced policy enforcement: A practical approach to defeat a wide range of attacks. In Proceedings of the USENIX Security Symposium, 2006.
8. Andreas Blass and Yuri Gurevich. Inadequacy of computable loop invariants. ACM Trans. Comput. Logic, 2(1):1-11, January 2001.
9. P. Cuoq, J. Signoles, P. Baudin, R. Bonichon, G. Canet, L. Correnson, B. Monate, V. Prevosto, and A. Pucceti. Experience report: Ocaml for an industrial-strength static analysis framework. In ACM SIGPLAN International Conference on Functional Programming, pages 281-286. ACM, 2009.
10. Chlipala. Static checking of dynamically-varying security policies in database-backed applications. In OSDI'10, Oct. 2010.
11. Fulton. Security through extensible type systems. SPLASH '12, pages 107–108, New York, NY, USA, 2012. ACM.

SEPS 2014: First International Workshop on Software Engineering for Parallel Systems

(Co-located with SPLASH 2014)

Ali Jannesari and Felix Wolf

German Research School for Simulation Sciences
RWTH Aachen University
{a.jannesari, f.wolf}@grs-sim.de

Walter F. Tichy

Institute for Program Structures and Data Organization Affiliation
Karlsruhe Institute of Technology (KIT)
tichy@kit.edu

Abstract

The first international workshop on Software Engineering for Parallel Systems (SEPS) will be held in Portland, Oregon, USA on October 21, 2014 and co-located with the ACM SIGPLAN conference on Systems, Programming, Languages and Applications: Software for Humanity (SPLASH 2014). The purpose of this workshop is to provide a stable forum for researchers and practitioners dealing with compelling challenges of the software development life cycle on modern parallel platforms. The increased complexity of parallel applications on modern parallel platforms (e.g. multicore, manycore, distributed or hybrid) requires more insight into development processes, and necessitates the use of advanced methods and techniques supporting developers in creating parallel applications or parallelizing and reengineering sequential legacy applications. We aim to advance the state of the art in different phases of parallel software development, covering software engineering aspects such as requirements engineering and software specification; design and implementation; program analysis, profiling and tuning; testing and debugging.

Categories and Subject Descriptors
D.1 [**PROGRAMMING TECHNIQUES**]: Concurrent Programming
D.2 [**SOFTWARE ENGINEERING**]
D.3 [**PROGRAMMING LANGUAGES**]

General Terms
Algorithms, Design, Languages

Keywords
Parallel programming, software engineering, parallel systems, multicore, manycore

1. Introduction

Parallel architectures e.g. multicore/manycore processors are common nowadays and parallelism is available almost on every

SPLASH '14 Companion, Oct 20-24 2014, Portland, OR, USA
ACM 978-1-4503-3208-8/14/10.
http://dx.doi.org/10.1145/2660252.2663602

machine. Unfortunately, many software products implemented sequentially fail to exploit potential parallelism out of parallel architectures. The goal of the workshop is to present a stimulating environment where topics relevant to parallel software engineering can be discussed by members of the SPLASH community and software and languages researchers. The intention of the workshop is to initiate collaborations focused on solving challenges introduced by ongoing research in the parallel programming field. Through Q&A sessions, presenters have the opportunity to receive feedback and opinions of other domain experts as well as to discuss obstacles and promising approaches in current research. Both authors and attendees can discover new ideas and new directions for parallel programming research.

The format of the workshop will be a full-day mini-conference. We welcome original, unpublished regular papers (12 pages) on current research, and industrial papers and tool presentations (short papers, 5 pages) as well as position statements (2 pages). We also intend to publish accepted papers in a special issue of the Elsevier Journal of Systems and Software (JSS), called Software Engineering for Parallel Systems, which JSS has agreed to host.

2. Topics of Interest

Specific topics of interest include, but are not limited to:

- Process models for parallel software development
- Requirement engineering of parallel software
- Design and build of parallel programs
- Parallel design patterns
- Parallel software architectures
- Modeling techniques for parallel software
- Parallel programming models and paradigms
- Profiling and program analysis
- Dynamic and static analysis
- Refactoring and reengineering for parallelism
- Performance tuning and auto-tuning
- Testing and debugging of parallel applications
- Tools and environments for parallel software development
- Case studies and experience reports

3. Organizers

Ali Jannesari (primary organizer) is the head of the multicore programming group at the German Research School for Simulation Sciences and RWTH Aachen University in Germany. His research interest is mainly focused on software engineering for multicore systems, including automated testing and debugging of parallel programs, parallelism discovery and parallelization methods, auto-tuning, and parallel programming models. Performing empirical studies towards the challenges that multicore developers are facing is another major interest of his. Jannesari has a PhD in computer science from Karlsruhe Institute of Technology. He is a member of the IEEE Computer Society, the ACM, and the German Computer Science Society. He was the co-organizer for the international EuroPar 2013 Parallel Processing conference in Aachen, Germany. He is responsible for the majority of the organizational aspects of the workshop. He is the primary contact and can be reached at jannesari@grs-sim.de.

Walter F. Tichy has been professor of Software Engineering at the Karlsruhe Institute of Technology (formerly University of Karlsruhe), Germany, since 1986, and was dean of the faculty of computer science from 2002 to 2004. Previously, he was senior scientist at Carnegie Group, Inc., in Pittsburgh, Pennsylvania and served six years on the faculty of Computer Science at Purdue University in West Lafayette, Indiana. His primary research interests are software engineering and parallelism. He is currently concentrating on empirical software engineering, tools and languages for multicore computers, and making programming more accessible by using natural language for programming. He earned an M.S. and a PhD in Computer Science from Carnegie Mellon University in 1976 and 1980, resp. He is director at the Forschungszentrum Informatik, a technology transfer institute in Karlsruhe. He is co-founder of ParTec, a company specializing in cluster computing. He has helped organize numerous conferences and workshops. He received the Intel Award for the Advancement of Parallel Computing in 2009. Dr. Tichy is a fellow of the ACM and a member of GI and the IEEE Computer Society. Contact him at tichy@kit.edu.

Felix Wolf is head of the Laboratory for Parallel Programming at the German Research School for Simulation Sciences in Aachen and a full professor at RWTH Aachen University, where he teaches parallel programming. His research concentrates on parallel programming tools. In particular, Wolf is a principal designer of the performance-analysis tool Scalasca, which is installed at numerous HPC centers around the world and which has been successfully applied to optimize academic and industrial codes. Wolf has published more than 90 refereed articles in journals and conference or workshop proceedings. He has obtained research funding from European and American funding agencies including BMBF, DFG, DOE, EU, Helmholtz Association, and NSF. He was the primary organizer of the international EuroPar 2013 Parallel Processing conference in Aachen, Germany. He is responsible for the reviewing process. Contact him at f.wolf@grs-sim.de.

4. Program Committee

The arrangement with PC members is already done and they are ready to serve as PC member in the workshop.

- Ehsan Atoofian (Lakehead University, Canada)
- Daniel Becker (Siemens AG, Munich, Germany)
- Siegfried Benkner (University of Vienna, Austria)
- Jeremy Bradbury (University of Ontario Institute of Technology, Canada)
- Jeffrey Carver (University of Alabama, USA)
- Clemens Grelck (University of Amsterdam, Netherlands)
- Christoph Kessler (Linköping University, Sweden)
- Victor Lee (Intel, CA, USA)
- Zhiyuan Li (Purdue University, USA)
- Pablo Oliveira (University of Versailles, France)
- Miquel Pericàs (Tokyo Institute of Technology, Japan)
- Michael Philippsen (University of Erlangen-Nuremberg, Germany)
- Michael Pradel (University of California, Berkeley, USA)
- Bernhard Rumpe (RWTH Aachen University, Germany)
- Massimo Torquati (University of Pisa, Italy)
- Shmuel Ur (University of Bristol, UK)
- Josef Weidendorfer (Technische Universität München, Germany)

5. Review Process

All submitted papers will receive at least three reviews. Authors of each accepted paper will have 30 min (including 5 min discussion) to present their work.

6. Invited Speakers

The workshop is also enriched by three confirmed invited talks presenting their ideas and interesting topics of the related fields. The invited speakers are:
- Michael Pradel (University of California, Berkeley)
- Jeffrey Carver (University of Alabama)
- Frank Schlimbach (Intel)

Acknowledgments

SEPS 2014 is organized with the support of the German Research School for Simulation Sciences (GRS) in Aachen, Germany. Also we would like to thank Workshop Chairs of SPLASH 2014 Stephanie Balzer and Du Li from Carnegie Mellon University for their support.

TD 2014: Workshop on Technical Debt in a World of Big Data and Big Teams

Dennis Mancl

Member of Technical Staff
Alcatel-Lucent
dennis.mancl@alcatel-lucent.com

Steven Fraser

Independent Consultant
Research Relations & Tech Transfer
sdfraser@acm.org

Abstract

Technical debt is an unavoidable part of software development in today's fast-paced market, but it is ignored by many of the people who should care about it most.

In large systems, a portion of the accumulating technical debt is just "sloppy design" caused by schedule pressure and other project forces. But the most important part of technical debt is directly related to project size and data complexity. How much technical debt is about large development teams and geographical distribution? How do current "big data" techniques (Hadoop, NoSQL, parallel algorithms, MapReduce) relate to technical debt issues?

This workshop explored strategies for understanding the impact of technical debt. If we believe that technical debt is an important issue in long-term software product development, do we have ways to keep the technical debt from causing development gridlock?

Categories and Subject Descriptors K.6.3 [**Software Management**]: Software maintenance – economics of evolving software; K.4.3 [**Organizational Impacts**]: Reengineering.

General Terms Design, Management.

Keywords Technical debt; agile development.

1. Technical Debt Plus "Big"

Big development creates big management issues and big technical issues. We have been using the "technical debt" metaphor to understand many issues in the evolution of large and small code bases. In this workshop, the workshop participants extended some of the things we have learned from the "agile development" world. To what extent can practitioners and managers on big projects learn from the experiences in "learning curve costs" of small data and small teams?

Technical debt is a term that was coined by Ward Cunningham in 1992 [1] to explain the accidental complexity that is a side-effects of "going faster" in the development work on a large code base.

Technical debt is a popular and powerful metaphor for small teams, projects with very short development cycles, and teams working in agile ecosystems, but it can apply to development projects of any size or circumstances.

This workshop examined the sources of technical debt, especially in the world of "big" software engineering. What are the best practices for keeping technical debt under control? The workshop participants shared both academic and industrial experiences.

This workshop explored these topics:

- Discipline: Is there a connection between following disciplined software engineering practices and low levels of technical debt?

- System impact: What is the impact of technical debt on achieving or failing to achieve good security or high reliability?

- Delivery: How does the presence of extra accidental complexity in a large system affect the ability to ship products on schedule?

- The impact of big: What kinds of technical debt are inevitable just because of a project's size and complexity?

- Visibility of technical debt in project planning: How should developers and managers plan for technical debt repayment? Are there simple models to help justify the "return on investment" in technical debt reduction efforts?

- Future: Will technical debt be a bigger issue five years from now than it is today?

SPLASH '14 Companion, Oct 20-24 2014, Portland, OR, USA
ACM 978-1-4503-3208-8/14/10.
http://dx.doi.org/10.1145/2660252.2663599

Technical debt is related to many other classic software engineering challenges. Technical debt is a kind of "accidental complexity," which is a concept originally discussed by Fred Brooks in 1987 [6]. Accidental complexity is the complexity related to design and implementation choices in the software solution that are not inherent in the problem. Accidental complexity is more widespread in large software systems.

In addition, data migration issues are always critical in long-lived applications. In the world of "big data", the challenges for application developers are greater – working not just with "old big data" instead of just "old data." Technical debt is connected to both architectural and organizational issues. In large software products built by large and complex organizations, there are many technical debt problems that are a result of a system structure that is parallel to the organization structure.

Some other useful discussions of technical debt issues can be found in [2], [3], [4], and [5].

2. Organizers

- Dennis Mancl, Alcatel-Lucent, Murray Hill, NJ, USA
- Steven D. Fraser, Independent Consultant, San Jose, CA, USA
- Bill Opdyke, Naperville, IL, USA

3. Post-workshop Poster

A post-workshop poster summarizing the most significant ideas shared and questions generated during the session is posted on the workshop website:

http://manclswx.com/workshops/splash14/index.html

References

[1] Ward Cunningham, "Technical Debt" article and video about the Technical Debt metaphor on the Portland Patterns Wiki site, http://c2.com/cgi/wiki?WardExplainsDebtMetaphor.

[2] Technical Debt online community website: http://www.ontechnicaldebt.com.

[3] SPLASH 2013 Workshop on Technical Debt final report: http://manclswx.com/workshops/splash13/final_report.html

[4] Eltjo R. Poort, "Driving Agile Architecture with Cost and Risk," *IEEE Software*, September-October 2014, pp. 20-23.

[5] Philippe Kruchten, Robert L. Nord, Ipek Ozkaya, Joost Visser, "Technical debt in software development: from metaphor to theory," *ACM SIGSOFT Software Engineering Notes*, September 2012, pp. 36-38.

[6] Frederick P. Brooks, "No Silver Bullet: Essence and Accidents of Software Engineering, *IEEE Computer*, April 1987, pp. 10-19.

WOSC 2014: Second Workshop on Optimizing Stencil Computations

Shoaib Kamil

MIT CSAIL

skamil@csail.mit.edu

Saman Amarasinghe

MIT CSAIL

saman@csail.mit.edu

P. Sadayappan

Ohio State University

sadayappan.1@osu.edu

Abstract

The second Workshop on Optimizing Stencil Computations is held in Portland, Oregon, USA on October 20, 2014, as part of the 2014 ACM SIGPLAN conference on Systems, Programming Languages, and Applications: Software for Humanity (SPLASH). The workshop's objective is to bring together users of stencil computations and building systems, languages, and frameworks that optimize such computations, which appear in a large variety of domains. Because of their ubiquity, importance, and relative simplicity, stencils are a rich and varied area of research for a number of systems communities, and we have constructed the workshop to emphasize cross-project discussion. In addition to submitted papers, we are inviting keynote speakers from important stakeholders who use stencils in their applications. Proceedings will be published in the ACM Digital Library [1].

Categories and Subject Descriptors   D [0]: General software

Keywords   Stencil computations, optimization

1.   Introduction

Stencil computations describe an important computational pattern that appears in a large variety of applications, including image processing, physical simulation, and linear algebra solvers. Because of their importance and wide usage, much effort is devoted to optimizing these kinds of computations on hardware that ranges from the largest supercomputers to handheld devices such as smartphones. Though conceptually simple, these computations have been traditionally difficult for general compilers to optimize, due to their difficult-to-analyze dependence structure and because the computations span many domains, each with different requirements for optimization and different tradeoffs. Thus, much of the real-world code used for stencil computations is hand-optimized for a particular application on a particular piece of hardware.

In recent years, a number of efforts have tried to automatically optimize stencil computations using general compilers, code generators, domain-specific languages, run-time systems, just-in-time compilation, and other strategies. This workshop aims to bring together these efforts along with users of stencils that require optimization to further the state of the art and promote a variety of research strategies for this important domain.

2.   Areas of Interest

Topics of interest include, but are not limited to, the following:

- memory and computational characterization of stencil applications
- benchmarking
- domain-specific optimizations, languages, and compilers for stencils
- polyhedral stencil optimization
- optimization of stencils for accelerators and other hardware
- parallel & distributed stencil optimization
- general compiler support for optimizing stencils
- code generation & auto-tuning for stencils
- static analysis, synthesis & verification of stencil computations
- high-level libraries & frameworks
- frameworks, languages, & optimizations for composing stencils
- multigrid & AMR-specific stencil optimizations

3. WOSC Program

WOSC 2014 will be a one day workshop held on October 20, 2014 in conjunction with SPLASH 2014 in Portland, Oregon. Presentations will consist of 20 minute talks and 10 minute discussions.

4. Organizers & Program Committee

4.1 Organizers

- Shoaib Kamil, MIT CSAIL, USA
- Saman Amarasinghe, MIT CSAIL, USA
- P. Sadayappan, Ohio State University, USA

4.2 Program Committee

- Matthias Christen, Universita della Svizzera Italiana
- David Keyes, King Abdullah University of Science and Technology (KAUST)
- Jonathan Ragan-Kelly, Stanford
- Brian Van Straalen, ANAG/Lawrence Berkeley National Laboratory
- Samuel Williams, Lawrence Berkeley National Laboratory

References

[1] ACM Digital Library, http://dl.acm.org

SPLASH 2014 Workshop Chairs' Summary

Following its long-standing tradition, SPLASH 2014 hosted 14 high-quality workshops, allowing their participants to meet and discuss research questions with peers, to mature new and exciting ideas, to build communities, and to start new collaborations. SPLASH workshops complement the main tracks of the conference by providing meetings with smaller and more specialized settings. Workshops cultivate new ideas and concepts for the future, which may or may not be recorded in formal proceedings.

The 14 workshops were selected out of 15 submissions. This year we employed, for the first time, a two-phase submission process, with early and late submission deadlines. This allowed us to accommodate workshops that wished to publish their proceedings in the ACM Digital Library as well as to consider relatively short-notice workshop submissions, while maintaining a high-quality reviewing process. We are very grateful that our program committee members supported this new process, even though it imposed a higher workload. We would like to express our gratitude to all the PC members: Sophia Drossopoulou, Thomas Gross, David Grove, Robert Hirschfeld, Shan Lu, Indrajit Roy, Mario Wolczko, and Peng Wu.

The workshops received great interest, with 287 registered participants overall, and 20 participants on average. The 14 workshops and their foci are listed below; the 8 workshops that published formal proceedings are identified.

- Fourth International SIGPLAN Workshop on Programming based on Actors, Agents, and Decentralized Control (AGERE!): The AGERE! workshop focuses on programming systems, languages and applications based on actors, active/concurrent objects, agents and—more generally—high-level programming paradigms, promoting a mindset of decentralized control in solving problems and developing software. (Published proceedings.)
- Second Workshop on Domain-Specific Language Design and Implementation (DSLDI): The goal of the DSLDI workshop is to bring together researchers and practitioners interested in sharing ideas on how DSLs should be designed, implemented, supported by tools, and applied in realistic application contexts.
- Domain-Specific Modeling workshop (DSM): An upward shift in abstraction leads to a corresponding increase in productivity. In domain-specific modeling (DSM), the models are constructed using concepts that represent things in the application domain, not concepts of a given programming language. This workshop brings together DSM researchers from industry and academia. (Published proceedings.)
- Foundations of Object-Oriented Languages (FOOL): The search for sound principles for object-oriented languages has given rise to much research during the past two decades. This workshop includes language semantics, type systems, memory models, program verification, formal calculi, concurrent and distributed languages, database languages, and language-based security issues.
- The Future Programming Workshop: this workshop aims to build a community of researchers and practitioners exploring the frontiers of programming, in particular, it looks for new ideas that could radically improve the practice of programming.
- Eclipse Technology eXchange (ETX): The Eclipse platform was originally designed for building an integrated development environment for object-oriented applications. The goal of the ETX workshop is to bring together researchers and practitioners to exchange ideas about

potential new uses of Eclipse and how Eclipse technology can be leveraged, improved, and/or extended for research and education. (Published proceedings.)

- Mobile Development Lifecycle (MobileDeLi): The mobile domain presents new challenges to software engineering. This workshop aims at establishing a community of researchers and practitioners to share their work and lead further research in the mobile development area. (Published proceedings.)

- Fifth Workshop on Evaluation and Usability of Programming Languages and Tools (PLATEAU): Programming languages exist to enable programmers to develop software effectively. But how efficiently programmers can write software depends on the usability of the languages and tools that they develop with. The aim of this workshop is to discuss methods, metrics and techniques for evaluating the usability of languages and language tools. (Published proceedings.)

- Second Workshop on Programming for Mobile and Touch (PROMOTO): Today, new programming languages are emerging to enable programmers to develop software easily. PROMOTO brings together researchers who have been exploring new programming paradigms, embracing the new realities of always connected, touch-enabled mobile devices. (Published proceedings.)

- The First International Workshop on Privacy and Security in Programming (PSP): This workshop seeks to enable the development of safe software systems by getting the people of these currently isolated fields to start talking, working together and addressing this very difficult issue. (Published proceedings.)

- Reactive and Event-based Languages & Systems (REBLS): This workshop gathers researchers in reactive and event-based languages and systems. The goal of the workshop is to exchange new technical results and to define better the field by coming up with taxonomies and overviews of existing work.

- Software Engineering for Parallel Systems (SEPS): The goal of the workshop is to present a stimulating environment where topics relevant to parallel software engineering can be discussed by software and languages researchers. The intention of the workshop is to initiate collaborations focused on solving challenges introduced by ongoing research in the parallel programming field.

- Workshop on Technical Debt (TD): This workshop explores strategies for understanding the impact of technical debt. If we believe that technical debt is an important issue in long-term software product development, do we have ways to keep the technical debt from causing development gridlock? The workshop discusses some approaches to taking on technical debt for systems at any scale.

- Workshop on Optimizing Stencil Computations (WOSC): Stencil computations describe an important computational pattern that appears in a large variety of applications, including image processing, physical simulation, and linear algebra solvers. This workshop aims to bring together these efforts along with stencils users that require optimization to further the state of the art and promote a variety of research strategies for this domain. (Published proceedings.)

We are very happy that the SPLASH workshops were so successful. We thank all the participants for their contributions and for being part of this community!

Stephanie Balzer   **Du Li**
Workshop Co-Chair   *Workshop Co-Chair*
Carnegie Mellon University   *Carnegie Mellon University*

A Summary of the First International Workshop on Software Engineering for Parallel Systems

Ali Jannesari and Felix Wolf

German Research School for Simulation Sciences
RWTH Aachen University
{a.jannesari, f.wolf}@grs-sim.de

Walter F. Tichy

Institute for Program Structures and Data Organization Affiliation
Karlsruhe Institute of Technology (KIT)
tichy@kit.edu

Abstract

This paper presents a brief summary of the first international workshop on Software Engineering for Parallel Systems (SEPS). The SEPS 2014 is held on October 21, 2014 in conjunction with the ACM SIGPLAN conference on Systems, Programming, Languages and Applications: Software for Humanity (SPLASH 2014) in Portland, Oregon, USA. The purpose of the workshop is to provide a stable forum for researchers and practitioners dealing with compelling challenges of the software development life cycle on modern parallel platforms. The increased complexity of parallel applications on modern parallel platforms (e.g. multicore, manycore, distributed or hybrid) requires more insight into development processes, and necessitates the use of advanced methods and techniques supporting developers in creating parallel applications or parallelizing and reengineering sequential legacy applications. We aim to advance the state of the art in different phases of parallel software development, covering software engineering aspects such as requirements engineering and software specification; design and implementation; program analysis, profiling and tuning; testing and debugging.

Categories and Subject Descriptors
D.1 [**PROGRAMMING TECHNIQUES**]: Concurrent Programming
D.2 [**SOFTWARE ENGINEERING**]
D.3 [**PROGRAMMING LANGUAGES**]

General Terms
Algorithms, Design, Languages

Keywords
Parallel programming, software engineering, parallel systems, multicore, manycore

SPLASH '14 Companion, Oct 20-24 2014, Portland, OR, USA
ACM 978-1-4503-3208-8/14/10.
http://dx.doi.org/10.1145/2660252.2694749

1. Introduction

Parallel architectures e.g. multicore/manycore processors are common nowadays and parallelism is available almost on every machine. Unfortunately, many software products implemented sequentially fail to exploit potential parallelism out of parallel architectures. The goal of the workshop is to present a stimulating environment where topics relevant to parallel software engineering can be discussed by members of the SPLASH community and software and languages researchers. The intention of the workshop is to initiate collaborations focused on solving challenges introduced by ongoing research in the parallel programming field. Through Q&A sessions, presenters have the opportunity to receive feedback and opinions of other domain experts as well as to discuss obstacles and promising approaches in current research. Both authors and attendees can discover new ideas and new directions for parallel programming research.

The format of the workshop was a full-day mini-conference. Presentations are made from 9:00 AM to 5:00 PM with breaks and 1-hour lunch break. We had overall 12 presentations: 9 presentation of the original, unpublished regular papers on current research, and 3 invited talks from keynote speakers. Accepted papers are considered to be published in a special issue of the Elsevier Journal of Systems and Software (JSS), called Software Engineering for Parallel Systems, which JSS has agreed to host.

2. Topics of Interest

Specific topics of interest include, but are not limited to:

- Process models for parallel software development
- Requirement engineering of parallel software
- Design and build of parallel programs
- Parallel design patterns
- Parallel software architectures
- Modeling techniques for parallel software
- Parallel programming models and paradigms
- Profiling and program analysis
- Dynamic and static analysis
- Refactoring and reengineering for parallelism
- Performance tuning and auto-tuning
- Testing and debugging of parallel applications
- Tools and environments for parallel software development
- Case studies and experience reports

3. Organizers

Ali Jannesari (primary organizer) is the head of the multicore programming group at the German Research School for Simulation Sciences and RWTH Aachen University in Germany. His research interest is mainly focused on software engineering for multicore systems, including automated testing and debugging of parallel programs, parallelism discovery and parallelization methods, auto-tuning, and parallel programming models. Performing empirical studies towards the challenges that multicore developers are facing is another major interest of his. Jannesari has a PhD in computer science from Karlsruhe Institute of Technology. He is a member of the IEEE Computer Society, the ACM, and the German Computer Science Society. He was the co-organizer for the international EuroPar 2013 Parallel Processing conference in Aachen, Germany. He is responsible for the majority of the organizational aspects of the workshop. He is the primary contact and can be reached at jannesari@grs-sim.de.

Walter F. Tichy has been professor of Software Engineering at the Karlsruhe Institute of Technology (formerly University of Karlsruhe), Germany, since 1986, and was dean of the faculty of computer science from 2002 to 2004. Previously, he was senior scientist at Carnegie Group, Inc., in Pittsburgh, Pennsylvania and served six years on the faculty of Computer Science at Purdue University in West Lafayette, Indiana. His primary research interests are software engineering and parallelism. He is currently concentrating on empirical software engineering, tools and languages for multicore computers, and making programming more accessible by using natural language for programming. He earned an M.S. and a PhD in Computer Science from Carnegie Mellon University in 1976 and 1980, resp. He is director at the Forschungszentrum Informatik, a technology transfer institute in Karlsruhe. He is co-founder of ParTec, a company specializing in cluster computing. He has helped organize numerous conferences and workshops. He received the Intel Award for the Advancement of Parallel Computing in 2009. Dr. Tichy is a fellow of the ACM and a member of GI and the IEEE Computer Society. Contact him at tichy@kit.edu.

Felix Wolf is head of the Laboratory for Parallel Programming at the German Research School for Simulation Sciences in Aachen and a full professor at RWTH Aachen University, where he teaches parallel programming. His research concentrates on parallel programming tools. In particular, Wolf is a principal designer of the performance-analysis tool Scalasca, which is installed at numerous HPC centers around the world and which has been successfully applied to optimize academic and industrial codes. Wolf has published more than 90 refereed articles in journals and conference or workshop proceedings. He has obtained research funding from European and American funding agencies including BMBF, DFG, DOE, EU, Helmholtz Association, and NSF. He was the primary organizer of the international EuroPar 2013 Parallel Processing conference in Aachen, Germany. He is responsible for the reviewing process. Contact him at f.wolf@grs-sim.de.

4. Program Committee

- Ehsan Atoofian (Lakehead University, Canada)
- Daniel Becker (Siemens AG, Munich, Germany)
- Siegfried Benkner (University of Vienna, Austria)
- Jeremy Bradbury (University of Ontario Institute of Technology, Canada)
- Jeffrey Carver (University of Alabama, USA)
- Clemens Grelck (University of Amsterdam, Netherlands)
- Christoph Kessler (Linköping University, Sweden)
- Victor Lee (Intel, CA, USA)
- Zhiyuan Li (Purdue University, USA)
- Pablo Oliveira (University of Versailles, France)
- Miquel Pericàs (Tokyo Institute of Technology, Japan)
- Michael Philippsen (University of Erlangen-Nuremberg, Germany)
- Michael Pradel (University of California, Berkeley, USA)
- Bernhard Rumpe (RWTH Aachen University, Germany)
- Massimo Torquati (University of Pisa, Italy)
- Shmuel Ur (University of Bristol, UK)
- Josef Weidendorfer (Technische Universität München, Germany)

5. Review Process

All accepted papers received at least three reviews. Authors of each accepted paper had 30 min (including 5 min discussion) to present their work. For this, we would like to thank all PC members for their time and helpful contributions.

6. Invited Speakers

The workshop is also enriched by three invited talks presenting their ideas and interesting topics of the related fields. The invited speakers were:

- Michael Pradel (University of California, Berkeley): "Automatic and Precise Program Analyses for Reliable and Efficient Concurrency"

- Jeffrey Carver (University of Alabama): "Applying Software Engineering Principles to Computational Science"

- Frank Schlimbach (Intel): "Dependence Programing with CnC "

Acknowledgments

SEPS 2014 is organized with the support of the German Research School for Simulation Sciences (GRS) in Aachen, Germany. Also we would like to thank Workshop Chairs of SPLASH 2014 Stephanie Balzer and Du Li from Carnegie Mellon University for their support.

REBLS'14 – 2014 Workshop Reactive and Event-based Languages & Systems (Post Conf. Workshop Summary)

Guido Salvaneschi

Technische Universität Darmstadt,
Germany
salvaneschi@cs.tu-darmstadt.de

Wolfgang De Meuter

Vrije Universiteit Brussel,
Belgium
wdmeuter@vub.ac.be

Patrick Eugster

Purdue University, USA; Technische
Universität Darmstadt, Germany
eugster@cs.tu-darmstadt.de

Lukasz Ziarek

State University of New York, USA
lziarek@buffalo.edu

Abstract

Reactive programming and event-based programming are two closely related programming styles that are becoming ever more important with the advent of advanced HCI technology and the ever increasing requirement for applications to run on the web or on collaborating mobile devices. A number of publications about middleware and language design – so-called reactive and event-based languages and systems – have already seen the light, but the field still raises several questions. For example, the interaction with mainstream language concepts is poorly understood, implementation technology is in its infancy and modularity mechanisms are almost totally lacking. Moreover, large applications are still to be developed and patterns and tools for developing reactive applications is an area that is vastly unexplored. This workshop gathers researchers in reactive and event-based languages and systems. The goal of the workshop is to exchange new technical research results and to define better the field by coming up with taxonomies and overviews of the existing work.

Categories and Subject Descriptors D.3.3 [*Programming Languages*]: Language Constructs and Features

Keywords Reactive Programming; Event-based Programming; Complex Event Processing; Functional Reactive Programming; Language Design; Object-oriented Programming

SPLASH '14,   October 20–24, 2014, Portland, OR, USA..
Copyright is held by the owner/author(s).
ACM 978-1-4503-3208-8/14/10.
http://dx.doi.org/10.1145/2660252.2694747

1. Introduction

The idea to conceive software as a suite of handlers that are registered in order to react on some changing entity is becoming ever more important. This is an indirect consequence of technological developments such as the advent of ever richer input devices (e.g., touch screens, multitouch tables, Kinects and other gesture-based technologies) and the fact that distribution in the form of peer2peer or web technology is becoming the default runtime environment. The challenge is to keep the application reactive at all times. Unfortunately, existing mainstream computational paradigms are not very fit for this task. They typically require the programmer to register a bunch of reaction procedures (a.k.a. observers, listeners, event-handlers, continuations, callbacks) with some potentially changing entity or with some globally accessible event broker. In order to keep the application reactive, these reaction procedures need to be short-lived procedures that refrain from iteration, recursion and calling other procedures as much as possible. Moreover, since calling other procedures is avoided, the reaction procedures typically communicate by means of global variables or variables that are in their surrounding scope. This is known as the inversion of control problem and the callback hell [3].

The difficulties resulting from this clumsy programming style have recently given rise to dedicated (a) event-based programming constructs that are added to or implemented in some existing programming language, and (b) a completely different computational paradigm (often referred to as reactive programming). In reactive programming programs are conceived as expressions that are automatically updated whenever one of their subexpressions is updated, and approach that originated in data-flow languages and functional-reactive programming. We refer to [4] and [1] for an overview of the field.

2. Topics of Interest

Even though reactive programming and event-based programming are receiving ever more attention, the field is far from mature. This workshop has the goal of joining forces and try to gather researchers working on the foundational models, languages and implementation technologies. Solicited contributions relate to topics that may include but are not restricted to:

- Study of the paradigm: interaction of reactive and event-based programming with existing language features such as object-oriented programming, mutable state, concurrency.

- Advanced event systems, event quantification, event composition, aspect-oriented programming for reactive applications.

- Functional-reactive programming, self-adjusting computation and incremental computing.

- Applications, case studies that show the efficacy of reactive programming, and empirical studies that motivate further research in the field.

- Patterns and best-practices.

- Related fields, such as complex event processing, reactive data structures, view maintenance, constraint-based languages, and their integration with reactive programming.

- IDEs, Tools.

- Implementation technology, virtual machine support, compilers. Modularity and abstraction mechanisms in large systems.

- Formal models for reactive and event-based programming.

3. Goals

The goal of the workshop is to create better cohesion in the community working on reactive and event-based programming, propose new solutions and come up with a clearer understanding of the boundaries of the field. We used the late afternoon session to discuss and exchange ideas about the fundamental paradigmatic problems that still need to be solved in order to reconcile reactive technologies with mainstream paradigms.

4. REBLS Program

The workshop has been organized as a mini-conference. Participants presented their work in slots of 1/2 hours; Q&A included. We successfully encouraged authors to use their 1/2 slots for presenting their work also based on live demos.

4.1 Keynote

Elm: Functional Reactive Programming for Front-End Applications (Evan Czaplicki) Elm [2] is a functional language for interactive graphics such as web apps, games, and visualizations. It is built around the ideas of immediate-mode rendering and Functional Reactive Programming (FRP). We will use Elm as a way to understand FRP and contextualize it in a broader taxonomy of reactive programming approaches. My goal is to illustrate:

The strong connection between pure functional programming and "immediate mode" rendering. How Elm's version of FRP guides the architecture of all programs, requiring a clean separation of model and view. The simplicity of Elm's FRP is a key factor in making it easy to write maintainable front-end code. How Elm fits into the broader taxonomy of reactive programming approaches, from message-passing concurrency to synchronous programming languages.

Bio Evan is the designer and lead developer of the Elm programming language. He works at Prezi where his role is to make Elm (the compiler, tooling, community, resources, etc.) great as a language and as a practical tool for commercial users.

4.2 Accepted Papers

Structured Reactive Programming with Céu, Francisco Sant'Anna, Roberto Ierusalimschy and Noemi Rodriguez (Departamento de Informática – PUC-Rio, Brazil) Structured synchronous reactive programming (SSRP) augments classical structured programming (SP) with continuous interaction with the environment. We advocate SSRP as viable in multiple domains of reactive applications and propose a new abstraction mechanism for the synchronous language Céu: Organisms extend objects with an execution body that composes multiple lines of execution to react to the environment independently. Compositions bring structured reasoning to concurrency and can better describe state machines typical of reactive applications. Organisms are subject to lexical scope and automatic memory management similar to stack-based allocation for local variables in SP. We show that this model does not require garbage collection or a free primitive in the language, eliminating memory leaks by design.

Taking Back Control (Flow) of Reactive Programming, Sean McDirmid (Microsoft Research Beijing, China) Event-driven programming avoids wasting user and CPU time, but is difficult to perform since program control flow is necessarily inverted and twisted. To ease reactive programming, many advocate burying control flow within abstractions that are composed via data flow instead. This might be a mistake: data-flow has challenges in expressiveness and usability that might not pan out. Instead, control flow could be re-invented to hide the adverse affects of CPU time while preserving expressiveness and directness.

Optimizing Distributed REScala, Joscha Drechsler and Guido Salvaneschi (Technische Universität Darmstadt, Germany) Reactive applications continuously adapt their internal state as a reaction to input events. In the Object-oriented paradigm, callbacks have been used to enable modular composition of reactive modules – often in form of the observer design pattern. Reactive Programming allows software composition through self-updating variables, referred to as behaviors or signals. As a result, code quality of reactive applications can be improved as code bloat from using explicit callbacks becomes obsolete.

Recently, motivated by the frequent use of callbacks in distributed systems, we advanced reactive programming to the distributed setting. In this paper, we present several optimizations for Distributed REScala, our solution for distributed reactive programming. After describing the details of each optimization, we present performance benchmarks that confirm the validity of our approach.

Archipelago: A Research Platform for Component Interaction in Distributed Applications, Eric Seckler and Robert Hirschfeld (Hasso Plattner Institute, University of Potsdam, Germany)   Distributed applications consist of different parts, which interact across distribution boundaries to achieve a common goal. The complexity of these interactions can vary within a single application and different interaction tasks require different mechanisms to communicate, coordinate, or share data or computation. We propose and evaluate Archipelago, our research platform to investigate and better understand object-oriented interaction in distributed applications. Archipelago is based on a shared object space that is replicated between application parts, a replication technology adopted from the Croquet project. We evaluate Archipelago by implementing illustrative examples and argue that our approach allows application parts to conveniently share structured data and computation and enables the implementation of reusable and extensible interaction mechanisms.

A Performance Enhancement Advisor for Event Processing Queries, Joong-Hyun Choi, Eun-Sun Cho and Chungnam (Nat'l Univ. Daejeon, Republic of Korea)   Recent event stream processing systems such as Esper, Oracle Complex Event Processing (CEP), and MS StreamInsight show practically acceptable performance. However, although it seems good news to the programmers writing reactive programs based on events, those systems do not work well on some types of queries yet, so that programmers should be careful about that. In addition, some of those systems take no measure about such queries, except publishing reference manuals telling programmers for themselves to avoid those queries, which aggravates burdens in reactive programming. In this paper, we propose an improved querying module for event stream processing systems, which helps programmers by giving them the hints to improve performance whenever their queries fall in any possible bad formats in the performance sense. We expect that our proposed module would be a big help to increases productivity of writing reactive programs where debugging, testing, and performance tuning are not straightforward.

Solving Interactive Logic Puzzles With Object-Constraints – An Experience Report Using Babelsberg/S for Squeak/Smalltalk, Maria Graber, Tim Felgentreff, Robert Hirschfeld (Hasso Plattner Institute University of Potsdam Potsdam, Germany) and Alan Borning (University of Washington Seattle, USA)   Logic puzzles such as Sudoku are described by a set of properties that a valid solution must have. Constraints are a useful technique to describe and solve for such properties. However, constraints are less suited to express imperative interactions in a user interface for logic puzzles, a domain that is more readily expressed in the object-oriented paradigm. Object constraint programming provides a design to integrate constraints with dynamic, object-oriented programming languages. It allows developers to encode multi-way constraints over objects and object collections using existing, object-oriented abstractions. These constraints are automatically maintained at run-time. In this paper we present an application of this design to logic puzzles in the Squeak/Smalltalk programming environment. We argue that our implementation facilitates event-driven applications with constraints on different parts of the system, by moving the burden to maintain the constraints from the developer to the runtime environment.

Alea Reactive Dataflow: GPU Parallelization Made Simple, Luc Bläser (University of Applied Sciences, Rapperswil Institute for Software), Daniel Egloff (QuantAlea Inc., Zurich), Oskar Knobel, Philipp Kramer (University of Applied Sciences, Rapperswil Institute for Software), Xiang Zhang(University of Applied Sciences, Rapperswil Institute for Software) and Daniel Fabian (InCube Group Inc. Zurich)   Making effective use of the GPU parallel power requires relatively complex and tedious work: Understandably, most programmers spare the efforts. The Alea reactive dataflow programming model now aims to substantially lower this threshold by simplifying GPU parallelization quite radically. Programs are described as data that is asynchronously propagated through a graph of operations, each typically predestined for vector parallelization. Programmers do no longer need to write GPU-specific code but instead leave the GPU- parallelization to the runtime system. Due to the declarative and reactive paradigm, operations can be easily scheduled as parallel streams on a GPU with minimum memory copying overheads.

5. Conclusion

We believe that the topic of the workshop is highly relevant to Splash participants. Reactive programming is a topic that exists for quite a number of years now (going back to FRP in the nineties) but which has received some incidental attention in our community as well. At the same time, the Advanced Modularity community at AOSD has been spending quite some effort on event-based programming. The topics have always been related. As indicated in the introduction, we believe that technological evolution will drive a need for the software engineering community to come up with solid knowledge on the topic.

6. About the Organizers

Guido Salvaneschi is a postdoc researcher at the Technical University of Darmstadt. His current research interests focus on programming language design of reactive applications, such as event-based languages, dataflow languages and functional reactive programming. His work includes the integration of different paradigms, incrementality and distribution. He obtained his PhD from Dipartimento di Elettronica e Informazione at Politecnico di Milano, under the supervision of Prof. Carlo Ghezzi with a dissertation on context-oriented programming and language-level techniques for adaptive software. Some of Guido's recent publications appear in OOPSLA'14, FSE'14, Modulariy'13 and Modularity'14, DEBS'14, IEEE Software. He served in the PC of MODULARITY'14 and FOAL'14 and co-organized the REM'13 workshop at SPLASH'13.

Wolfgang De Meuter is a professor at the Vrije Universiteit Brussel. He leads a research group that is working on ambient-oriented programming, distributed middleware, RFID-enabled applications, cloud-oriented programming techniques, participatory sensing and reactive programming. He is the author of numerous publications in programming language engineering and won the Dahl-Nygaard Junior prize in 2008. He has been active in organizing several workshops at ECOOP and OOPSLA. He was the workshop chair of ECOOP'05 and the PC-Chair of Coordination'11. He took the initiative to organize the ECOOP workshop series on Object-oriented Language Design for the Post-Java Era which was the direct precursor of the Revival of Dynamic Languages workshop series which finally ended up in the Dynamic Languages Symposium at Splash. He has served on several PCs of Splash and Ecoop.

Patrick Eugster is an Associate Professor of Computer Science at Purdue University where he leads the Distributed Programming Group. Patricks area of expertise lies in the intersection of programming languages and distributed systems. Some of Patricks recent publications appear in ECOOP'12, ICDCS'12, DSN'12, Sensys'11, OOPSLA11, and Middleware'11. He was PC co-chair for DEBS'12. He has served on several PCs for conferences like ECOOP, ICDCS, and Middleware. Patrick is a recipient of a NSF CAREER award among others. His work has been supported by NSF, DARPA, Northrop Grumman, Purdue Research Foundation, Google, and Amazon. He served as workshop (co-)chair of ECOOP'08 and '12. Patrick co-organized a successful SPLASH'10 workshop on Programming Support Innovations for Emerging Distributed Applications.

Lukasz Ziarek has received his Ph.D. in Computer Science from Purdue University in May 2011. He is working at the University at Buffalo the State University of New York as an Assistant Professor. He serves on the advisory board and is the acting President of Fiji Systems Inc. located in South Bend, Indiana. He has served on the program committees of HILT'14, JTRES'14, DAMP'12, JTRES'11, and JTRES'10 and is the general chair of JTRES'14. He has helped organize the local CSTA annual conference, Python workshops for HS teachers, and was the chair of the SPLASH'13 and SPLASH'14 Doctoral Symposium.

Acknowledgments

The successful edition of the workshop would have never been possible without the help of the program committee members. We thank them for their precious work. Jonathan Edwards (MIT), Philipp Haller (Typesafe), Hridesh Rajan (Iowa State University), Chiba Shigeru (University of Tokyo), Dominique Devriese (Katholieke Universiteit Leuven).

This work has been supported by the German Federal Ministry of Education and Research (Bundesministerium für Bildung und Forschung, BMBF) under grant No. 01IC12S01V and by the European Research Council, grant No. 321217.

References

[1] E. Bainomugisha, A. L. Carreton, T. v. Cutsem, S. Mostinckx, and W. d. Meuter. A survey on reactive programming. *ACM Computing Surveys*, 45(4):52:1–52:34, Aug. 2013.

[2] E. Czaplicki and S. Chong. Asynchronous functional reactive programming for GUIs. In *Proceedings of the 34th ACM SIGPLAN Conference on Programming Language Design and Implementation*, PLDI '13, pages 411–422, New York, NY, USA, 2013. ACM.

[3] L. A. Meyerovich, A. Guha, J. Baskin, G. H. Cooper, M. Greenberg, A. Bromfield, and S. Krishnamurthi. Flapjax: A programming language for ajax applications. In *Proceedings of the 24th ACM SIGPLAN Conference on Object Oriented Programming Systems Languages and Applications*, OOPSLA '09, pages 1–20, New York, NY, USA, 2009. ACM.

[4] G. Salvaneschi and M. Mezini. Reactive behavior in object-oriented applications: An analysis and a research roadmap. In *Proceedings of the 12th Annual International Conference on Aspect-oriented Software Development*, AOSD '13, pages 37–48, New York, NY, USA, 2013. ACM.

TD 2014: Workshop on Technical Debt in a World of Big Data and Big Teams

Dennis Mancl

Member of Technical Staff
Alcatel-Lucent
dennis.mancl@alcatel-lucent.com

Steven D. Fraser

Independent Consultant
Research Relations & Tech Transfer
sdfraser@acm.org

Abstract

Technical debt is an unavoidable part of software development in today's fast-paced market, but it is ignored by many of the people who should care about it most. Technical debt is more often swept under the rug. This workshop explored the issues of debt mitigation and management. We discussed the most important techniques for making technical debt visible, and also addressed what we need to teach others about technical debt issues.

Categories and Subject Descriptors K.6.3 [**Software Management**]: Software maintenance – economics of evolving software; K.4.3 [**Organizational Impacts**]: Reengineering.

General Terms Design, Management.

Keywords Technical debt; agile development.

1. Technical Debt

Technical debt is a term that was coined by Ward Cunningham in 1992 [1] to explain the accidental complexity that is a side-effects of "going faster" in the development work on a large code base.

Technical debt is a popular and powerful metaphor for small teams, projects with very short development cycles, and teams working in agile ecosystems, but it can apply to development projects of any size or circumstances.

This workshop examined the sources of technical debt, especially in the world of "big" software engineering. What are the best practices for keeping technical debt under control? The workshop participants shared both academic and industrial experiences.

SPLASH '14 Companion, Oct 20–24, 2014, Portland, Oregon, USA.
ACM 978-1-4503-3208-8/14/10.
http://dx.doi.org/10.1145/2660252.2696499

2. Mitigating Technical Debt

In big projects, we need strategies for keeping technical debt under control, and sometimes to prevent creating it in the first place. The most important strategies to keep technical debt from growing are:

- Avoid duplication, especially "forking" existing code
- Keep a list of technical debt issues: a kind of "technical debt backlog"
- Use the most experienced development team available
- Use scenario-based modeling to supplement the feature lists and defect lists that usually drive development projects

Duplicated code always contributes to a longer learning curve and increased maintenance costs. By keeping a list of technical debt issues, it is easier to "make payments" (including some design and code improvements in the project schedule). Although it isn't always possible to build a team of experienced staff for every project, it is certainly possible for a team to invest some time in learning: to become a more experienced over time. Scenario-based modeling helps developers think about the overall architecture and focus on the essential improvements.

3. Managing Technical Debt

All software development teams need to invest time and effort in finding technical debt problems. Some potential problems can be identified with tools, such as static analysis tools (Coverity, Klockwork, Sonar, and others). These automated tools are very good at finding duplicated code and violations of coding style rules. But these tools only find some of the technical debt problems in a large code base.

There is also a role for manual problem finding methods: design reviews and code reviews. We look for design shortcuts, poorly structured class interfaces, and undisciplined use of dynamic references. Some of these issues might be fixed immediately and others might be added to the technical debt backlog.

Are there some simple measures that managers should track to understand how serious technical debt costs might be? There are three practical ways to assess the impact of technical debt:

- Estimate how much the build/test/deploy cycle is slowed down by technical debt issues

- Estimate the total amount of time to fix all items in the technical debt backlog

- Compare the results of performance tests and load tests from one iteration to the next

4.   What do we teach to the next generation?

Young developers need to get early experience with technical debt. Of course, it is impossible to learn anything about technical debt by doing solo development (the most common development model in education). Every young developer needs to have multiple experiences working as part of a team of five or six developers: reviewing designs and code written by others, adding code to an existing software system where the original developers are not available, getting practice with static code analysis tools, and working with the other team members to select the most important refactoring opportunities.

Unfortunately, it can be very difficult for instructors and students to set up this "ideal" learning experience. Outside of a course with teams working on a big semester-long project, are there other ways to get some experience with technical debt issues?

One useful way to learn about design collaboration is to participate in a Design Fest. This is a single three-to-five hour session where a team of four to six developers collab-orate to create a design for a simple problem. In past years, some software conferences such as OOPSLA would have a Design Fest session that would assign volunteers to small design teams, and most of the teams would post their final designs on the Internet for comparison. See http://designfest.acm.org for some examples of Design Fest structure and some suggestions for design problems.

Hackathons and mashup sessions can also be used to get some team-based implementation experience, Although most hackathon projects are relatively simple and usually involve minimal formal programming, there are many opportunities to explore technical debt issues as part of the design process.

In addition to getting direct development experience, it is very important for young developers to get some experience in refactoring techniques. Refactoring is a skill that requires both knowledge and practice to do it well.

5.   Post-workshop poster

A post-workshop poster summarizing the most significant ideas shared and questions generated during the session is posted on the workshop website:

http://manclswx.com/workshops/splash14/index.html

References

[1] Ward Cunningham, "Technical Debt" article and video about the Technical Debt metaphor on the Portland Patterns Wiki site, http://c2.com/cgi/wiki?WardExplainsDebtMetaphor.

[2] Technical Debt online community website and blog: http://www.ontechnicaldebt.com.

[3] SPLASH 2013 Workshop on Technical Debt final report: http://manclswx.com/workshops/splash13/final_report.html

[4] Philippe Kruchten, Robert L. Nord, Ipek Ozkaya, Joost Visser, "Technical debt in software development: from metaphor to theory," *ACM SIGSOFT Software Engineering Notes*, September 2012, pp. 36-38.

Author Index